ALSO BY SIDNEY RUTBERG • TEN CENTS ON THE DOLLAR

THE
MONEY
BALLOON

Inflation and How to Live with It

by

SIDNEY RUTBERG

SIMON AND SCHUSTER · NEW YORK

Designed by Eve Metz
Manufactured in the United States of America

1 2 3 4 5 6 7 8 9 10

Library of Congress Cataloging in Publication Data

Rutberg, Sidney.
   The money balloon.

    1. Inflation (Finance)—United States. 2. Investments—United
States. I.Title.
HG538.R84   322.4′1′0973   74–28359
ISBN 0–671–21990–1

TO MY MOTHER AND THE MEMORY OF MY FATHER

CONTENTS

THE
MONEY
BALLOON

I

INFLATION

REFLECTIONS IN THE SEAT OF MY PANTS

Inflation has been built into our economy and will probably remain as much a part of the American Way of Life as television commercials, frozen French-fried potatoes and traffic jams. A little inflation usually accompanies high employment, economic growth and rising corporate profits. The trick is to keep a little inflation from developing into a lot of inflation.

The only cure known to man for inflation is a rip-roaring, hair-curling, old-fashioned depression. Such anti-inflation measures as tight money and high taxes are effective only to the extent that they move the economy toward a recession. Price controls are no more than cosmetic—but don't underrate the power of a good make-up job. For illusion is one of the charms in perpetuating inflation. There are illusory profits, illusory pay increases and illusory growth, all of which are psychologically more satisfying than no profits, no raises and no growth.

Modern inflation comes in two basic styles—demand-pull and cost-push. Demand-pull is the garden variety, with too much money chasing too few goods. This fits in with all the classical theories based on neatly charted supply/demand curves. Money increases demand, and if supply doesn't keep pace, prices go up. All nice and simple.

Cost-push inflation doesn't follow the charts. No less an economic authority than Ludwig Erhard, who took postwar Germany from shambles to prosperity, was completely puzzled by the U.S. economy in 1969–70 when unemployment was rising, sales were slipping because of a slowdown in demand, yet prices were rising.

"I can't understand how you can have a recession and inflation at the same time," he told a group of visiting American journalists in the summer of 1970.

But the American economists explained the phenomenon and called it cost-push inflation. In our economy, the pricing structure was not a clear-cut function of supply and demand.

With only four corporations manufacturing cars and one computer company with 70 per cent of the market, free competition was not around to push prices down when the demand weakened. There was also big labor. The unions were getting increases for members even though business was lousy. When the labor unions got theirs, unorganized labor generally got more money too.

When the costs of doing business went up, so did prices. This development came as an affront to classical economic thought, which held that costs had nothing to do with prices. According to the textbooks, you were supposed to sell your products at the prices set in the market place, and if you lost money, you just quietly went out of business and left the market to the more efficient producers. Well, American free enterprise is not all that free, and business was not ready to sacrifice its profits just to satisfy the prejudices of a bunch of chart-drawing theoreticians.

A more dramatic instance of cost-push inflation came at the end of 1973 when the oil-exporting nations got together

INFLATION   13

and decided they had been selling their product too cheaply. They quadrupled the price of oil. As a bloc, the exporting nations had a monopolistic position, and free-market supply/demand factors in pricing could be ignored. A monopolist fixes his prices at the point of optimum return to himself. The world needs oil, we have the oil, so we'll charge what we think will do us the most good.

Since energy is at the core of any industrial society and oil is a principal source of energy, the cost-push impact was enormous. The United States, which used to worry about inflation rates of 5 or 6 per cent, suddenly found itself faced with double-digit inflation—over 10 per cent. Countries like Italy and Japan, which had to import almost all their oil, had to deal with even higher rates—about 17 per cent in Italy and 25 per cent in Japan.

Fuel costs have an all-pervasive effect on an industrial economy, since there is no productive effort that doesn't depend on energy. Rents go up because fuel costs rise; electric bills go up as utilities pass on their increased costs to consumers; steel goes up to cover increased energy costs; autos go up to cover higher steel costs, etcetera ad infinitum.

The energy-related inflation was especially difficult to deal with since traditional inflation-fighting policies wouldn't help much. Tight money or higher domestic taxes would not bring down the cost of oil, but if the money policy was tight enough or the taxes high enough, they could bring on a depression.

In February of 1974, the United States joined the world of double-digit inflation, hitting 10 per cent. The Organisation for Economic Cooperation and Development (OECD) reported that for the 12 months ended February, only 7 nations of the 24-nation organization were in the one-digit range. Germany had the best record at 7.6 per cent. The other members of that increasingly exclusive club were Canada, Norway, Holland, Austria, Belgium and Luxembourg.

At the other end of the inflation spectrum were Greece with 33.4 per cent and Japan with 26.3. Britain was at 13.2, France 11.5. Even Switzerland, the very essence of monetary integrity, suffered a 10 per cent inflation rate.

By April, Canada joined the double-digit group with an inflation rate averaging 11 per cent for the 12-month period. Belgium also went double-digit at 11.6 per cent, while Sweden was back with the singles at 8.6 per cent and Switzerland squeaked in at 9.9 per cent.

It was hoped that the price increases spawned by the leap in oil costs would prove to be what economists called "soft core" inflation. That is, an essentially one-shot deal that would work its way through the world economy and then quit. Meanwhile, the oil exporters, who felt that world-wide inflation was eroding the real value of their increased profits, threatened to charge even more for their product if the rest of the world didn't get inflation under control. This the economists termed *chutzpah*.

Another inflationary force in the 1973–74 surge was commodity speculation. Reuters index of basic commodities soared nearly 200 per cent from the fall of 1971 to March, 1974. Much of the increases can be attributed to a world-wide shortage of basic commodities, but speculation surely aggravated the situation. When prices are rising, the speculators will push them higher; when prices are falling, speculation will add downward pressure.

I can see no justification for accountants to be buying sow bellies or advertising men bidding up the price of fish meal when their speculative influence could mean a peasant or African tribesman will be priced out of his daily food ration. There should be a blanket prohibition against speculating in vital commodities without a genuine business purpose. A flour mill should be buying wheat futures and a candy manufacturer, cocoa futures; but a pediatrician's buying soybeans merely creates a false indication of demand. If the speculators must play games, let them buy gold and silver and old Superman comic books.

While cost-push inflation is relatively new, inflation itself is as old as prostitution. The Mesopotamians had it in 2000 B.C., the Greeks had it and the Romans had it. Inflation was so severe in Rome that in the year 301 A.D., the Emperor Diocletian went so far as to institute a full-blown program of price and wage controls. It didn't work worth a damn, even though the penalty for violating the price ceilings was death. After a couple of years the entire program was scrapped because it was impossible to administer.

In our own history, inflation was an important issue dating back to the days of the American Revolution and the Continental Army. The Americans used the printing presses to finance the Revolution, and by 1780 Continental currency and currency issued by the individual states was worth only one-fortieth of its face value. This gave birth to the cliché about things' not being worth a continental.

In the nineteenth century there were several other periods of inflation fueled by land speculation. These were inevitably followed by busts, or panics as we were wont to call them in those days.

The Civil War brought its own inflation, and it hit on both sides of the conflict. The North issued $450 million in greenbacks backed by nothing but a promise to pay, a promise made slightly suspect by the fact that the Government itself would not accept the greenbacks in payment of customs duties. (The Romans had tried to set this same type of monetary double standard when the emperors paid off in adulterated coins but refused to accept these coins for taxes.) The greenbacks plunged in value, and when the war ended you could get 74 greenbacks for a real dollar.

Meanwhile, down South the Confederacy was unable to collect the taxes it needed to finance the war, so it turned to bonds and notes and issued over $2 billion worth. By 1864 these bonds were down to 5 cents on the dollar—slightly better than the greenbacks—but by the time the War Between the States ended, the bonds were worth zilch. Prices took off, and in 1864 a barrel of flour went to $500, bacon to $8 a pound and candles $10 a pound. An effort by the government to fix prices met with the same lack of success the Romans had experienced more than 1,500 years earlier and President Nixon was to encounter more than 100 years later.

While Confederate money became worthless, the North's greenbacks were ultimately redeemed at 100 cents on the dollar. In 1875 the Government resumed paying gold for all paper currency, including greenbacks. This had the effect of reducing the outstanding greenbacks from $450 million to $300 million and helped bring on deflation as the economy expanded and the money supply remained constant.

Deflation, of course, is the opposite of inflation and results from an inadequate money supply. Prices decline and factories close and farmers plow under crops and its a mess.

I doubt that we'll ever see deflation again, partially because of a technology gap. The great technological breakthroughs we've made in the production of goods haven't nearly kept up with the quantum leaps that have been made in creating money. (See Running the Printing Presses in a Brooks Brothers Suit.)

In the post–Civil War period, farmers were screaming for greenbacks or at least for the free use of silver to inflate the money supply. To a farmer, deflation is deadly because he gets less money for his crops and must pay off his mortgage with increasingly expensive money. Since agriculture was at the heart of the American economy, when farmers screamed, politicians listened.

Over the next 65 years there were cross-of-gold speeches and free-silver parties and Greenback parties and Populist parties and assorted panics and finally the Great Depression of the 1930's, the most recent U.S. deflation. The experience of the 30's is probably still an important influence in a general bias toward inflation over deflation.

Reliance on monetary metals for a money supply works poorly because it locks the economy into a box whose dimensions are determined by the availability of one inert metal or another. A logical alternative is to adjust the money supply to the needs of the economy. This is precisely what the Federal Reserve Board has been trying to do, but it hasn't worked much better than the mindless metals.

The money supply, unfortunately, cannot be turned on and off by the Fed without some disturbing side effects. For starters, take interest rates.

If the money supply is curtailed to reduce inflation, interest rates will take off. High interest rates are anti-inflationary because they tend to discourage borrowing and take some of the steam out of an economy that's expanding too fast. At the same time, higher interest rates mean higher costs and higher costs mean higher prices and it's difficult for the layman to grasp the subtle difference between higher prices and inflation.

Economists don't see higher prices and inflation as synonymous because that's too simple. To them, inflation is the process of blowing up the money supply; deflation, or disinflation—a bit of Washingtonese designed to further muddle matters—is the process of letting the air out of the economy through contracting or slowing up the growth of the money supply.

In this century the all-time greatest example of inflation in an industrial state shattered Germany after World War I. This experience with inflation had much the same impact on the Germans as the Great Depression had on Americans. The Germans today still have a deadly fear of inflation, and since World War II West Germany has the best record among industrial nations of maintaining the purchasing power of its currency.

The modern Deutschemark came into being on June 20, 1948, when Germans stood in line at their banks to receive an allocation of 40 marks each. A few months later each German was issued another 20 marks.

World War II had so crippled the German economy that before the new currency was issued, cigarettes were used as the medium of exchange. Under the guidance of Ludwig Erhard, regarded as the architect of postwar Germany's remarkable economic renaissance, and with the help of massive U.S. Marshall Plan aid, the Germans got it all together, and in the 25 years from 1948 to 1973 the mark lost only 41 per cent of its purchasing power.

Only 41 per cent? Although that sounds horrendous and the Germans were by no means happy with it, their record was considerably better than Great Britain's 66 per cent, France's 72 per cent and Japan's 75 per cent, and somewhat better than the 45 per cent decline of the U.S. dollar.

The German inflation of the 1920's, while notable for its intensity, was a classic case of too much money racing after too few goods. The Germans, after being stripped of their territories, foreign investments, shipping fleets, railroad cars and other heavy transport equipment, were saddled with a staggering reparations bill of 132 billion marks (roughly $30 billion). In early 1921, when the reparations commission fixed the price, the value of the mark was 4.2 to the dollar. By May of that year the mark had fallen to 62 to the dollar. This decline continued and accelerated, and by the end of January, 1923, the mark had plunged to 40,000 to the dollar.

In January of 1923 the French and Belgians occupied the Ruhr, and the German government had the additional burden of paying striking workers and civil servants who had been expelled from the occupied territory. The German economy was at a standstill, except for the paper and printing plants. There were 300 factories working full time producing paper for the Reichsbank and 2,000 presses operating around the clock to print the bank notes.

Reparations installments were payable in dollars, forcing the German government to buy up dollars in the foreign-exchange markets at whatever price was demanded. Speculators moved into the market, adding their weight to the mark's dizzying descent.

Prices were going up every week, then every day, then every hour. Workmen were paid several times a day so that they could rush out and exchange their money for something of value before what little purchasing power was left dissolved in their hands. The foreign-exchange markets became the pricing mechanism for merchants, who would close their stores during trading hours and then return to raise their prices in line with the currency market. Some workers tried to beat the constantly rising prices by throwing their money out the windows to their waiting wives, who would rush to unload the nearly worthless paper. A postage stamp cost millions of marks and a loaf of bread, billions.

The inflation reached a climax in the month's delay between October 15, when the government decided to replace the Reichmark with the Rentenmark, and the actual issuance of the new currency. The delay was caused by a strike of government printers; before the new notes could be issued, the mark had ballooned from 25 million to the dollar to 4.2 trillion, and in Cologne, where the French and Belgian armies had moved in, the mark reached 11 trillion (11,000,000,000,000) to the dollar.

Rentenmarks were issued on the basis of 1 each trillion (1,000,000,000,000) of old marks, the exchange rate was fixed at 4.2 to the dollar and the new currency was backed by a mortgage on farm land and industrial estates.

While the Germans considered the Rentenmark caper an economic miracle in dealing with the rocketing inflation, the miracle ultimately led to deflation and an economic stagnation that set the stage for the rise of Hitler and World War II.

Thus the choice between inflation and deflation seems like

a choice between being stretched on a rack and being crushed by a heavy rock. Our modern industrial economies, in the main, have opted for a little bit of inflation rather than a little bit of deflation because of the tendency of inflation to go hand in hand with growing economic activity. And growth is an international hang-up.

But a little inflation can easily progress from a creep to a walk to a gallop, and governments around the world have been wrestling—mostly unsuccessfully—with the problem of containing inflation within reasonable limits. About the only success they've had is through the device of inflating the definition of "reasonable." In the 1960's an inflation rate of 1 or 2 per cent a year in the United States was considered reasonable. In the 70's "reasonable" has been blown up to about 5 per cent.

World-wide, the accelerating rate of inflation has put a severe strain on the redefiners. A study by the First National City Bank, published in September, 1973, shows that the purchasing power of the currency of industrialized nations was eroding at the rate of 7.3 per cent a year in the first seven months of 1973. (It has since accelerated.)

The average rate of currency depreciation has nearly doubled since the mid-1960's for industrial nations and more than tripled for the less developed nations.

For the industrialized countries the 1973 rate of depreciation ranged from 4.7 per cent in the United States to 16.7 per cent for Yugoslavia. Among less developed countries the range was from less than 1 per cent for Morocco to 41.7 per cent for Argentina.

Governments use two fundamental approaches for fighting inflation—fiscal policy and monetary policy. Fiscal policy has to do with government expenditures and taxes, and monetary policy deals with jerking around with the money supply.

Politically, it's safer for elected officials to have the money supply juggled than to mess with fiscal policy. The electorate at large has little grasp of monetary aggregates and M_1 and M_2 and the mysterious dealings of the Federal Reserve Banks in buying Treasury securities and then selling them back in open-market operations. The impact of a tight or loose monetary policy is something the voters read about on the financial pages but don't get very much excited about.

But higher taxes, that's a kick in the gut. You don't have to have a degree in advanced economic theory to see that your pay check is smaller because of increased withholding taxes. As for a cut in government spending—another facet of fiscal policy—its impact also is felt without the aid of a Ph.D. in money and banking. Lop off a Congressman's pet spending project and the screams of anguish can be heard clearly through the clicking of the voting machines.

Thus when inflation needs cooling off, the usual practice is to turn the job over to the bankers and their fancy book-keepers. This doesn't get at the root of inflation, and the basic economic infection continues to fester.

It is in the nature of us all to look for a system that will give us what we want without our paying the price. The most attractive of all economic theories is the Adam Smith laissez-faire approach. Let everyone follow his own self-interest and everything will work out just dandy. What could be more beautiful? It doesn't work.

Appealing to the same psychological search for the free lunch is the monetarist theory of economics. All you have to do to make everything come out right is increase the money supply at a constant rate—4 per cent a year or 5 per cent or 6 per cent—and the economy will move happily on its own and inflation will remain under control. The monetarists will tell you to the penny how much inflation you'll get at any fixed rate of money-supply increase—all other things being equal. All other things are never equal.

If the monetarist theory (some call it a religion) doesn't

work and an effective fiscal policy is politically impractical, how about price controls? They don't work either, but that doesn't mean they won't be used again and again. While I don't think the law of supply and demand stands up as well as the law of gravity, it certainly has an influence, and the trouble with price controls is that they are in essence a legislative effort to repeal a natural law.

There is one area in which price controls can be of some help in fighting inflation, but it is more a matter of public relations than economics. That's in dealing with inflationary expectations.

One way to beat inflation is to spend faster, emulating the German workers of the 20's, who threw their money out the windows so that there would be no time wasted in getting it spent. When prices are going up rapidly, what you buy today will be more expensive tomorrow. Thus inflation feeds on itself as the fear of higher prices becomes a cause of higher prices. Price controls that appear to be vigorously administered can have the effect of calming the fears of inflation, but only for a short period because as soon as a few cracks appear, massive disillusionment sets in.

A government lid on prices being pushed upward by supply/demand forces must breed distortions. In 1971, President Nixon, a great free-market enthusiast, nevertheless started a program of price controls when the popularity polls were screaming for something to be done about inflation. His action was political, since he disliked controls intensely. Phase One, a 90-day freeze, and Phase Two, a complex system of enforced price controls, worked pretty well largely because the underlying economy was slightly soft and prices were not pressing too hard against the ceilings.

Price controls work best when they're needed least. But when the economy is booming along and the momentum of prices is strongly upward, controls break down as black markets and shortages appear. The Nixon program was aided in its collapse by some administrative bumbling on Phase Three, a program that was billed as "voluntary" but that was supposed to carry a stick in the closet with which to beat nonvolunteers. Confusion in the business community was massive, and Phase Three had to be supplanted with another freeze—but by that time the whole system had deteriorated to the point of no return. Phase-out was the only remaining alternative.

Price controls also stir up strong outcries from free-market types who abhor this tampering with the beauty and symmetry of supply/demand. But periodically price controls are used, and they will continue to show up because governments must give the appearance of action.

In answer to the question "Why don't they do something about this terrible inflation?" government must do something. And when prices are rising faster than income, the politicians are not likely to vote a tax increase to take some of the pull out of demand. Instead, price controls become the ultimate solution.

The Romans had the same fundamental economic problems nearly 2,000 years ago that we have today and experimented with price-wage controls when the going got really rough.

The Romans had constant wars in outlying districts that kept military budgets and taxes high, closely paralleling our own wars in Korea and Vietnam. The government payrolls were padded with hordes of soldier-agents whose principal function was the extortion of bribes. (Libel laws inhibit the discussion of modern American counterparts.)

The Romans used money to buy off the barbarians. They offered cash payments in exchange for nonaggression pacts and at times were paying as much to the barbarians as they paid to support Roman armies.

As the barbarians grew stronger and the Romans weaker, the Romans made deals to buy victories. The barbarians acquiesced to nominal defeats in exchange for cash. This type of thing is not too far removed from our offers of aid to North Vietnam; the only half-joking suggestions during the Vietnam War that we declare ourselves the victors and leave; and finally, the "peace with honor" that permitted U.S. soldiers to leave Vietnam while we continued to supply South Vietnam's army. The war continued.

But back to the Romans. Debasement of coinage—using base metals in coins—was big among the Roman emperors in their effort to get the most mileage out of the available silver and gold. This rather unsophisticated use of monetary policy began in the early days of the Empire, and scholars have traced it as far back as Nero, who fiddled and ruled in the middle of the first century A.D. But in the third century coin debasement became a national pastime. The higher the cost of government, the greater was the need for adulterated coins. The coins got so bad that the government that issued them refused to accept them as tax payments.

It was a messy state of economic affairs that greeted Diocletian when he became Emperor in 284 A.D. He reformed the tax system and introduced a new currency to replace the old inflated coins in circulation, but inflation persisted.

The costs of constant wars and the maintenance of the Roman army—which had increased from 300,000 men to 400,000—plus the cost of a huge government bureaucracy and the upkeep of the royal court, brought on a new wave of inflation. It was for this reason that in the year 301 A.D., Diocletian instituted a system of price and wage controls.

Diocletian's move was unprecedented in Roman history, and to make sure the controls would work, the emperor proclaimed that violations of the price or pay ceilings, or withholding products from the market or hoarding, would be punishable by death. Talk about a stick in the closet!

In a proclamation that could have been written by a Madison Avenue or Washington public relations man, Diocletian made it clear that he was most unhappy with the measure, but was forced to take such drastic action because of "the excesses perpetrated by persons of unlimited and frenzied avarice." He went on to lament that "human forbearance" that might have righted the "cruel and pitiable situation" came out a poor second to the "desire of these uncontrolled madmen . . . to have no thought for the common need."

Since the market place would not provide a solution, concluded the Emperor, he, as protector of the common good, must step in:

> We hasten, therefore, to apply the remedies long demanded by the situation, satisfied that no one can complain that our intervention with regulations is untimely or unnecessary, trivial or unimportant. These measures are directed against the unscrupulous, who have perceived in our silence of so many years a lesson in restraint but have been unwilling to imitate it. For who is so insensitive and so devoid of human feeling that he can be unaware or has not perceived that uncontrolled prices are widespread in the sales taking place in the markets and in daily life in the cities? Nor is the uncurbed passion for profiteering lessened by abundant supplies or fruitful years . . .

Within two years the "passion for profiteering" proved even more powerful than the threat of death, and the effort to control prices and wages was abandoned.

A Christian writer of the day, whose views may have been influenced by Diocletian's policy of persecuting Christians, described the price-control efforts in terms you might expect from a present-day Democratic economist evaluating a program of a Republican administration or a Republican economist writing about a Democratic effort:

> . . . when by various iniquities he [Diocletian] brought about enormously high prices, he attempted to legislate the prices of commodities. Then much blood was spilled . . . nothing appeared on the market because of fear and prices soared much higher. In the end,

after many people had lost their lives, it became absolutely necessary
to repeal the law.

Inflation is cruelest to those with fixed incomes, particularly the elderly living on pensions or modest savings. Remember those pictures that used to run in all the magazines
of the smiling old couple shown gracefully retired on "$200
a month"? They wouldn't be smiling much now on $200 a
month. Yet many old people must try to live on that kind of
income. The average monthly Social Security payment to
some 16 million Americans in mid-1974 was $186 a month.
And this princely sum was reached only after a 6.6 per cent
increase in January and a 4.5 percent raise in July of that
year.

In an effort to ease the pain somewhat, Social Security
payments are now geared to be increased automatically with
the cost of living, but the standard of living of many senior
citizens remains deplorably low. As a result of galloping inflation, some have taken to shoplifting. Supermarkets have
reported that as the price of food has risen, so has the inci-
dence of petty theft by oldsters trying to sneak an extra can
of tuna fish or a small package of meat.

Less dramatic, but still painful, is the squeeze of inflation
on the wage earner whose raises are more than eaten up by
rising prices, and even on the fat-cat corporations whose
ballooning expenses can outrun profits.

The trick in living in an inflationary period is to see that
your income goes up faster than the price level. In the
United States since World War II, the American worker, in
the main, has been keeping up. From 1950 to 1972, hourly
earnings of production workers went up 176 per cent while
consumer prices were rising 74 per cent. But since 1972,
price rises have accelerated and wages have not kept up.

Furthermore, as far as the consumer is concerned, it's the
bottom line that counts—what he has left to spend after

taxes—and a study by the Tax Foundation shows that the consumer has not done too well. During the period between 1966 and 1973, a family of four with a 35 per cent rise in income came out behind because of the tax bite and inflation.

The loss to inflation during that period was 36.6 per cent, so the 35 per cent income rise was chewed up immediately. But add to that the increase in taxes and there's a substantial net loss. A family with an income of $5,000 that increased to $6,750 wound up losing $140 in purchasing power, and the affluent family with an income of $50,000 that went to $67,500 suffered a drop in purchasing power of $3,286, according to the Tax Foundation's calculations.

I might point out that the 35 per cent income-increase figure chosen by the Tax Foundation was an arbitrary one and did not reflect the actual rise in personal income during that period. A check with the foundation's research department to determine the actual income increase during the period brought the response "We really didn't check into that too much, but the actual increase was probably higher than that. Probably 40 or 45 per cent."

A later report by the foundation showed that the wage earner's position had worsened. In the period from 1966 to 1974, the head of a family of four who had increased his earnings by 50 per cent—from $10,000 to $15,000 a year— had still lost $159 in purchasing power as a result of inflation and higher taxes. The $50,000-a-year executive who had worked his way up to $75,000 would have been behind by $2,477 in purchasing power.

This time, the survey pointed out that earnings of Federal employees and construction workers increased by almost 75 per cent during the period, so they were still ahead. But the earnings of millions of workers in wholesale and retail trade, in manufacturing and in some services did not keep up with the erosion of purchasing power.

What about the impact of inflation on corporate profits?

On the surface, it would seem that a moderate rate of inflation should automatically increase dollar profits, since the
sale of the same number of units would bring in more dollars
and thus more profits. But it doesn't work that way. During
a period of inflation a corporation's costs increase, often
faster than its own selling prices.

There's another kicker: inventory profits. The Morgan
Guaranty Trust Company of New York figured out that during the first half of 1973, a period when corporate profits rose
at an annual rate of better than 50 per cent, more than half
the increase came from higher inventory values. In an article titled "Phantom Profits," the bank maintains that inventory gains are really the worst kind of profits, since corporations must pay out cash for taxes on bookkeeping profits and
must pay higher financing costs to maintain the same unit
inventory.

"Rather than showing whopping increases," said Morgan
Guaranty, "after-tax profits net of inventory profits actually
declined in the first two quarters of this year . . . Indeed,
on that basis profits' share of gross national income is 43 per
cent below the average level of 1960's."

Before you start sending CARE packages to Corporate
America, let me add that Morgan Guaranty is a very snooty
bank that won't let anyone through the door in less than six
figures, and the tone of the article was more than slightly
defensive. High profits are always an embarrassment to Corporate America, especially during a period when the working staff is being battered by inflation.

But Morgan does have a point, and as further proof, First
National City Bank (not as snooty as Morgan but still with
some stake in corporate profits) cited Wall Street's reaction
to the 1973 profit rise. Robert E. Lewis, a Citibank vice-
president, in a talk in September, 1973, before the National
Association of Business Economists, pointed out that the
"quality" of corporate profits kept investors from bidding up

the price of stocks. He noted that profits had to be adjusted for the inflated dollar, inventory revaluation and the increasing cost of replacing equipment.

By fooling around with the figures, Lewis demonstrated it was possible to show profits in a range from up as much as 51 per cent to down as much as 29 per cent for the same period.

There is a school of thought that sees inflation as inevitable (I enrolled several years ago) and suggests that Americans just "relax and enjoy it." The Phillips curve, first published in November, 1958, by Professor A. W. Phillips of the London School of Economics, often is cited as proof that policy makers must choose between inflation and unemployment.

Actually, the Phillips curve measured the level of unemployment and changes in unemployment against wage rates. Using the experience of Britain over a period of nearly 100 years, Professor Phillips concluded that the more unemployment, the less pressure for wage increases. Since economists have been in the habit of blaming inflation on increasing labor costs, they were quick to conclude that the Phillips curve measured the trade-off between inflation and unemployment. The fear of unemployment and the political repercussions of a disenchanted labor force has tended to foster inflationary government policies.

Since the end of World War II, it has been the official policy not only of the United States but of the United Nations to foster full employment. Article 55 of the U.N. Charter states that all members shall promote full employment, and Article 56 says that this shall be an individual effort of members and a joint effort of the organization. If inflation rates are any indication of the enthusiasm with which U.N. members have accepted the challenge of full employment, this can be put down as one of the few successes of an otherwise impotent organization.

In the United States, Congress passed the Whittington-Taft Employment Act of 1946, a watered-down version of the Full Employment Bill.

Originally, the bill provided that it be a national policy to ensure continuing full employment and declared:

All Americans able to work and seeking work have the right to useful, remunerative, regular and full-time employment and it is the policy of the United States to assure the existence at all times of sufficient employment opportunities to enable all Americans who have finished their schooling and who do not have full housekeeping responsibilities freely to exercise this right.

The bill was defeated and instead Congress passed the Whittington-Taft measure, which aimed at "maximum" employment rather than "full" employment.

But full employment or maximum employment, our Government is committed to keeping as many people working as possible, consistent with a free-enterprise economy operating at maximum efficiency, and it's the job of the President's Council of Economic Advisers to provide the leadership in this undertaking. As a result, if Professor Phillips and his curve have any validity, the Employment Act fosters inflation.

International trade is another complication in trying to control inflation.

As tariff barriers come down and as world trade increases, control over domestic prices erodes. If we could build a wall around the United States and deal only with each other, we might maintain better control of domestic prices (they'd probably be much higher, but at least there wouldn't be any foreigners influencing our decisions). With things as they are, our inflation is exported overseas and inflation of our trading partners is exported to us.

In 1973 inflation was world-wide and there was no way the United States could be an exception.

Edgar R. Fiedler, then Assistant Secretary of the Treasury for Economic Policy, came before a group of businessmen in New York in September of 1973 to explain why an administration that had been talking about a 3 per cent inflation rate was now dealing with prices increasing at 8 or 9 per cent a year.

Fiedler said that the inflationary surge was largely the result of two factors: crop failure and an economic boom throughout the industrialized world.

"Global cereal production fell a disastrous 4 per cent from 1971 to 1972," said Fiedler. "Wet weather hurt the soybean harvest in the United States at the same time that the Peruvian anchovies disappeared. Similar supply shortfalls hit cotton and other farm commodities. Together, these difficulties created unprecedented pressures on farm and food prices."

Turning to the boom, Fiedler said:

"Perhaps never before have so many countries experienced such rapid growth in output at the same time. The inevitable result is a supply/demand imbalance in all major industrial raw materials and an unprecedented burst of price increases."

In sum, Fiedler was asking: What the hell could the Administration do about acts of God and other foreigners?

And as if the world-wide boom, crop failures and disappearing anchovies weren't enough, the stunning oil-price increases were tossed into this inflationary stew.

One of the holes in the price-control program of the early 70's was in the export field. Price ceilings applied to domestic prices but not to exports, so anyone with a choice of customers would naturally sell to the highest bidder—often the foreign buyer. Furthermore, at that time the dollar had been through a series of devaluations, and this gave the foreign buyer extra leverage. If you could get dollars cheaply, you could bid more of them for the merchandise you wanted.

Aside from the fundamentals of the world economy that impinge on our domestic economy, there are also international monetary gimmicks through which one country can export its inflation or unemployment to other nations.

Competitive devaluations and revaluations are traditional tools used by sovereign states to ship their economic ills to others.

Devaluation will make a nation's goods cheaper internationally, keep its workers employed and cause unemployment in the country that imports cheap merchandise. The cheap imports force domestic producers to shut down because they can't compete. Thus devaluation exports unemployment.

Inflation can be exported through revaluation—raising the value of one's currency in relation to other currencies. Imported goods become cheaper for the revaluing country, and this brings domestic prices down. Meanwhile, trading partners must pay more for the goods of the revaluer, and the importers' domestic prices rise.

Historically, devaluation was in fashion because the strategy was designed to maintain domestic employment at high levels and the supply/demand balance was weighted toward maintaining demand. In 1973, the pendulum swung sharply in the other direction as shortages multiplied and supply became the big problem. If shortages remain as a major concern, you can be sure that revaluations will become increasingly popular. Also, export controls will probably replace tariffs in this new environment of mounting demand and shrinking supply.

One of the advocates of the "relax and enjoy it" philosophy is Columbia University Professor Stefan H. Robock, a specialist in international business and Latin American studies. He says that a stable price level is a "second class myth" and in a *Harvard Business Review* article (November–December, 1972) cites the experience of Brazil, which has geared its economy to a high level of inflation by automatic adjustments. Brazil's inflation topped out at 91.6 per cent in 1964 and had been worked down to 15.7 per cent in 1972. Professor Robock's article contended that with a 20 per cent inflation rate in 1971, Brazil still had about the highest real growth rate of any country in the world and that this illustrated that by adjusting to inflation, Brazil can avoid sacrificing billions in production to anti-inflation measures.

The Brazilian economy, tightly managed by a military government, has been growing at a 10 to 11 per cent annual rate (vs. 4 or 5 per cent considered sustainable for the United States) after adjusting for inflation. In Brazil the entire economy floats upward with inflation through a system of escalating wages, rents, interest rates and pensions in line with cost-of-living increases.

Think-tank director Herman Kahn of the Hudson Institute compared the fight against inflation to the fight against drug addiction and prescribed indexing (the term used for the Brazilian formula) as a form of methadone treatment for inflation. Others have used the drug metaphor in opposing indexing. They see indexing as a drug that will require progressively larger doses to remain effective.

One of the biggest guns to join the pro-indexing ranks is University of Chicago economist Milton Friedman. He has stated that indexing would take some of the pain out of inflation. Furthermore, he regards indexing as "simply inevitable."

"The hard truth," said Dr. Friedman in one of his *Newsweek* columns,

is that we face continuing inflation at a substantial though uncertain rate. The hard truth is that it is extremely difficult for the ordinary man to protect himself from the ravages of inflation. The encouraging fact is that there are feasible innovations that would reduce the ravages of inflation. The sooner they are adopted the better.

The principal argument against indexing is that rather than cure, it perpetuates and intensifies inflation while reducing incentives to get at the root of the problem.

Gabriel Hauge, chairman of Manufacturers Hanover Trust Company, strongly attacked the concept in the bank's Special Report of January, 1974:

> I do not believe that this country can adjust itself, without great risk, to institutionalized, indexed price inflation. I see no practical way to protect the poor who rely on income support, the elderly who rely upon their savings to supplement Social Security benefits and many others. If there are people who benefit from inflation, they are the speculators we would not voluntarily choose to assist. Meanwhile, the innocent and helpless suffer. Moreover, I submit that our economic history does not support the proposition that growth cannot be achieved without inflation. Check the statistics for the golden year 1955.
>
> Our country, in spite of much that has been written to the contrary, is still work-oriented and devoted to the principle of thrift and savings. The vast majority of our people still believe in the proposition that they should make arrangements during their working lives to help provide for themselves in retirement, with private pensions and personal savings supplementing Social Security benefits. Price inflation must have adverse effects upon the savings ethic. Through that channel alone, it could have unpredictable results upon the entire fabric and fiber of our society.

Another inflation hawk, Alfred Hayes, President of the Federal Reserve Bank of New York, called indexing a "siren song" that "would prove very dangerous for this country." He said his most serious objection to such a plan was that "it would vastly weaken the country's resolve ever to bring inflation under control."

In addition to the philosophical objections to the Brazilian method, there have been some disquieting cracks appearing in the Brazilian economy, and there have also been reports that the Brazilians have been doctoring their statistics.

For 1973, Brazil officially reported an inflation rate of 15.5 per cent, some 3.5 percentage points above the government's 12 per cent target. And, according to The New York Times, government sources in Brazil privately conceded that 1973 inflation was really over 20 per cent.

In 1974, the increase in oil prices pushed other prices up painfully, since Brazil imports 80 per cent of its oil. For the first quarter, the Brazilian government, under what First National City Bank called a "truth in prices" policy, reported an increase in wholesale prices of 10.5 per cent, which translates into an annual rate of 42 per cent. The cost-of-living index of Rio de Janeiro increased by 16 per cent in the first four months of the year, or at an annual rate of 48 per cent.

Another factor in the "success" of the Brazilian program has been the acquiescence on the part of the laboring classes to a program that reduced the real wages of unskilled workers by about 30 per cent over the ten years to 1970. There was also increased concentration of wealth and a widening of the gap between the rich and the poor. In short, the Brazilians improved business and industry at the expense of labor.

There is a considerable gap between the economy of Brazil and that of the United States. Brazil is in the early stages of developing from an agricultural society into an industrial one; the United States is the world's leading industrial power. In 1973 Brazil had a Gross National Product of about $60 billion; the United States produced $1.29 trillion. The United States' GNP grew by $134 billion that year, a figure more than double the entire Brazilian output. Even after washing out inflation from our GNP figures (and not from the Brazilian), U.S. growth in that one year exceeded Brazil's total production of goods and services.

Government control is pervasive in the Brazilian economy. State-controlled corporations run most of the steel, mining, petroleum, energy and transportation industries. It was estimated that in 1974, 70 per cent of Brazil's investment represented government-controlled enterprises.

Finally, to adapt the Brazilian system to the United States would require frequent devaluations of the dollar. If the Brazilians devalue the cruzeiro every four or five weeks it's no big deal, but if the U.S. dollar were devalued at such frequent intervals, international finance could be seriously disrupted. There are some economists who feel that with floating exchange rates adjustments could be made smoothly. However, the dollar would be floating in uncharted waters.

But whether or not the indexing method can work in the United States, many of its features have gradually found their way into our economy.

· One economist who apparently didn't worry too much about inflation, at least prior to the oil crisis, was Leon M. Keyserling, Chairman of President Truman's Council of Economic Advisers from 1950 to 1953. Keyserling preached that growth is where it's at.

He says that worry over inflation has resulted in restrictive policies that have wasted billions in productive capacity. It is his contention that if we just keep on pumping money into the economy through Federal deficits and a smartly expansionary monetary policy, the increased production will add enough to supply to keep inflation from getting out of hand.

Writing in *The New York Times* of September 29, 1973, Keyserling said:

> The performance of the economy and the people's well-being are more important than a surplus or deficit in the Federal budget; besides, the preponderance of the recent deficits have been due to sorely deficient economic growth.

Keyserling decries the loss of production and gives his version of why prices were rising:

> Under current policies (Phase Four price controls, tight monetary policy and efforts to keep the Federal budget in balance), I estimate that we would forfeit during 1972–80 another 1.7 trillion dollars of total national production with corresponding losses of other types. This assuredly we cannot afford.
>
> Stagnation and recession cut the productivity growth rate enormously, increase *per unit* [italics his] labor costs, and prompt price increases.

In fighting inflation, the orthodox methods of tight monetary and fiscal policies are designed to slow the economy by cutting down on demand. Tight money and high taxes (or less government spending) will create unemployment and an economic climate in which price increases cannot be sustained because the consumer just doesn't have the money to pay higher prices.

This is a highly unsatisfactory method of containing inflation, but that's how it's done in the capitalist world. Differences are mostly in degree and in the mix of fiscal and monetary policy.

The tendency in the United States has been to lean more heavily on monetary manipulation because it's less visible to the voter than fiscal action. It is also less effective, takes a long time to take hold and is highly discriminatory in its impact.

The first to feel the sting of tight money are small businessmen who are turned down by banks in favor of larger borrowers who are better customers. No banker of sound mind would use scarce funds for loans to small, marginal customers at the risk of having to turn away a bigger, more credit-worthy borrower.

Tight money also focuses in on the housing industry, quickly drying up mortgage money and cutting off construction, particularly of residential housing. This spills over into the industries that supply the housing market, and step by step the money crunch washes over the entire economy.

On the other hand, an increase in a broad-based tax, such as the income tax, spreads itself through the economy much more evenly and with less delay. But the pain is sharper, and it's easy to identify the culprits who inflicted it.

The alternatives offered by Keyserling and Robock are much more appealing than either tight money or tax hikes. Why go through traumatic recessions or stagflations in order to keep inflation down to some arbitrary percentage? Instead we could just let the economy go full steam ahead and either adjust income and interest rates to keep pace or better still, as Keyserling sees it, keep the pressure up on the supply side until it eventually catches up with demand, at which point prices would level off.

My own feeling, based on what has happened inside my head from reading millions of words by economists, listening to a mind-numbing number of speeches and lectures and watching economic developments as they unfold, is that the "relax and enjoy it" school will prevail. Our economy is already building in the kind of adjustments that Professor Robock found so successful in Brazil and Professor Friedman sees as inevitable: escalator clauses in labor contracts tied to living costs; periodic increases in Social Security payments; floating interest rates on bank loans, mortgages and some forms of savings accounts. There will be more. All this amounts to a sort of seat-of-the-pants economics that is infinitely more effective than the rigidities of monetarism, fiscalism or any other form of economic orthodoxy. The eclectic pragmatist is astride the wave of the future, and somehow he'll help us all muddle through.

Paul A. Samuelson, MIT's Nobel Prize–winning professor of economics, author of the best-selling standard textbook on economics and a Big Three economist (the other two are Friedman and Galbraith), had this to say in an article on inflation appearing in the June, 1974, issue of the Morgan Guaranty Survey:

> One is forced by the facts of experience into an eclectic position. It is not a case where intellectual indecision or uncertainty leads to a hedged position of eclecticism. It is rather that explanation of the varied pattern of ongoing experience calls for bold combination of causations.

Now, this is not the kind of writing that will tempt students to forsake their frisbees and rush to Economics class (Dr. Samuelson's Nobel Prize was not for literature), but it appears to be a vote for the "muddling through" theory of economics.

In looking for protection against the ravages of inflation, the moneyed seek sure-fire refuges—real estate, works of art, antiques, wines, gold coins, stamps. Anything but money.

Any of these could make fine investments—but the investor must know what he's doing or an "inflation hedge" could chew up his cash the way a garbage-disposal unit eats chicken bones. Real estate can be highly profitable, but it also can bring quick disaster to the novice. Webb & Knapp and Glickman Corporation, two of the nation's largest real estate corporations, collapsed in bankruptcy, losing millions for investors. Other real estate operators who bought "income-producing property" in the Bronx or in downtown Newark, New Jersey, found out that tax losses are not always fun.

Works of art have increased tremendously in value, but the art market is a tricky business. An art investor with a limited income *may* pick the work of a young artist who becomes another Picasso. But chances are the artist will turn out to be just another bearded youngster who never should have left his father's hardware business in Scranton, Pennsylvania; his paintings will be as salable as the graffiti on the Lexington Avenue subway.

Even the affluent investor who can afford the work of an established artist will probably need a 100 per cent appreciation just to break even. There's a yawning spread between the bid and the asked price in the art market because the commission a gallery charges for selling a painting ranges from 35 to 50 per cent. So if you buy a painting for $25,000 and its value rises to $50,000, your profit might just cover the commission charge.

In the case of gold coins, there's a large premium over the value of the gold content. If gold is selling at $100 an ounce, coins containing an ounce of gold may cost twice that much.

Antiques have also been rising in price during the current inflation, but the distinction between antiques and secondhand furniture is a nebulous one.

In an article in *The New York Times Magazine* (June 10, 1973), Professor J. H. Plumb of Christ's College, Cambridge, described what he called England's "junk mania." England was in the midst of a raging inflation, and every village was dotted with signs proclaiming "antiques" for sale. At these village markets, he said, "for ludicrously high prices, one can buy what our parents consigned to the trash can."

This craze, Professor Plumb pointed out, was not confined to the villages but had invaded London's posh art galleries. "Even Christie's and Sotheby's are caught up in the fever. Old wine bottles, even old corkscrews, are soaring to $250 and, for rare ones, nearly $500."

Also being actively sold and traded as antiques were old postcards, photographs and broken toys. Professor Plumb concluded that never before had any nation had so much junk for sale as Britain.

Whether this "junk" will prove out as sound hedges against inflation is an open question, but I'm skeptical. Professor Plumb pointed out that back in the seventeenth century the Dutch went wild over tulip bulbs and bid prices up outrageously. How would you feel about having all your money tied up in tulip bulbs today?

There are two basic rules to follow for living in an inflationary environment: see that your income increases faster than prices and be a debtor rather than a creditor.

The advantage of being a debtor during inflation inspired the farmers to scream for free silver and greenbacks. At 1974's inflation rate, the $100 you borrow today will be repaid with the equivalent of $88 a year later. Borrowing is a bargain, and it makes sense to keep your home mortgaged to the rafters. Not only do you get a break on repayment of the mortgage, but inflation is likely to increase the value of your property.

Don't buy fixed-interest long-term bonds. The purchase of a bond puts you in the position of a creditor, and you'll be

on the receiving end of the depreciated money. Other rami-
fications of the business of bonds will be detailed in the
chapter on the stock market. Common stock, which represents ownership of assets and should be expected to increase
in value as money depreciates, has not followed this logical
path, for reasons that will be explored in the aforementioned
chapter.

Investment for profit can help, but there are no sure
things. Profitable investment requires specialized knowledge
or dumb luck—or ideally, a combination of both. Since dumb
luck is pretty much of a random phenomenon, we can at
least improve the odds by learning the business before putting our money on the line.

Increasing real income is difficult, and there is no magic
formula. It involves working harder, longer. It means more
members of the family go out and work. It means greater investment in education—professional or technical. While doc-
tors, lawyers and accountants complain as much as everyone
else about inflation, they're in an infinitely better position to
cope with it than the hourly worker or the clerk.

There are lots of dopey little tips for living with inflation,
ranging from planting your own back-yard vegetable garden
to making your own clothes to buying day-old bread to
riding a bicycle to work, but these are of minimal benefit. Even getting higher wages for doing the same job doesn't
help much, because the increase will soon be eaten up by inflation. If you get more money but aren't producing any
more, the higher pay rate is just pumping more air into the
money balloon. Nothing has been added to the economy to
justify more money for you, and it doesn't take too long before the economy realizes this and takes the raise away from
you.

II

GOLD

MAGIC MONEY OR LATRINE LINER
PAR EXCELLENCE

Gold is a form of primitive money that evolved after it was discovered that livestock made a mess around the house and iron was too bulky to carry around.

Gold is the prettiest of metals, it never rusts, its supply is limited but not too limited and it has been used for money for many thousands of years.

John Maynard Keynes, the British economist, called it a "barbarous metal," General Charles de Gaulle saw it as "the unalterable fiduciary value par excellence" and Nikolai Lenin thought gold should be used to decorate public toilets.

Wars have been fought over it, kingdoms toppled for lack of it and great new lands explored in search of it.

But gold is largely irrelevant in a modern industrial society in which untold billions of dollars in value are recorded on computers thousands of miles from the transactions and credit, not cash, plays the most vital role in commerce.

Throughout all history an estimated 80,000 to 100,000 tons of gold have been mined (three-quarters of it in this century), and at $42.22 an ounce—the official price—the entire world supply would be worth between about $95 billion and $120 billion. Central banks of the non-Communist world hold about $43 billion worth. In the United States alone, it has been estimated that the requirements for new capital during the period from 1974 to 1985 will be in the neighborhood of $3.3 trillion. Gold cannot support a capital explosion of that magnitude.

William McChesney Martin, when he was Chairman of the Federal Reserve Board, went along with Keynes in classifying gold as a "barbarous relic." At a 1968 conference, Martin outlined what has pretty much remained the U.S. position on gold:

Said Martin:

I have been quoted as saying that gold is a barbarous metal. But it is not gold that is barbarous; that wasn't my point. Quite the contrary; gold is a beautiful and noble metal. What is barbarous, when it occurs, is man's enslavement to gold for monetary purposes.

He then pointed out that history has shown

a steady progression away from exclusive dependence on gold as a monetary instrument. In very few countries now is gold any longer used domestically for monetary purposes—either as a medium of exchange or as a regulator of monetary policy. Supplements to and substitutes for gold have been developed and have taken over gold's role as a monetary asset.

Annual production of gold has been running at between $1 billion and $1.6 billion since 1950 (at the official price), with South Africa turning out about three-quarters of the non-Communist world's supply of newly mined gold. Canada is second with about 6 per cent, and the United States is third with about 4 per cent. The Soviet Union is a large gold producer and probably ranks second to South Africa, but figures on Soviet production are kept secret.

If the matter is looked at unemotionally, there is no need

for gold at all. If billions in goods and services can change hands on the trust of one party in the other, what do we need gold for? We dig it out of one hole, refine it, cast it into bars and then put it into another hole, all because of naive faith that gold is a permanent store of value and if everything else breaks down, we can always turn to gold. This works fine, as long as we never really have to look to gold for value—because if we did, we'd find we'd been kidding ourselves for all these years.

I remember talking to a Swiss banker about the fascination gold holds for Europeans. What was there about this metal that made it acceptable in exchange for everything from everyone? As far as I could see, it was an attractive metal with limited utility that was highly overrated.

He said he agreed with my appraisal. "You know gold is useless and I know it, but there is nothing else. It is important to maintain the fiction that gold has intrinsic value and universal acceptance because if the people lose faith in gold, there is nowhere else to go. If the dollar weakens we can buy German marks; if the pound weakens, we can buy dollars. But after gold there is nothing. Gold is the money of last resort."

Thus we find the fiction of gold's value serves as well as fact as long as we don't have to test it.

A subtopic of the fictional properties of gold is the illusion that gold or the gold standard will prevent inflation. By definition, inflation is the process of increasing the money supply, and since there is no way to increase the supply of gold at a rate faster than the South African mines can produce it, a gold standard will prevent inflation.

Under a gold standard, the reasoning goes, governments will be unable to create money. Paper money can be printed in unlimited amounts, and this puts governments in the position of running the printing presses at their whim and sending prices soaring. Governments and politicians are not to be trusted. Put your faith in gold, say the aficionados.

They're right about not trusting politicians and governments, but a dumb inert metal isn't going to help, because while politicians may not be trustworthy, they are clever. There is no difficulty in getting around the disciplines gold is supposed to enforce.

As far back as history goes, the practice of increasing the money supply by adding a little lead to the gold or scraping some of the gold off the edges of coins has been commonplace.

But dilution and coin scraping are relatively crude methods of raising money, and if they were the limits to which politicians were held, gold would indeed place a discipline on governments. However, even the ancients could figure out innovative methods of outsmarting the system.

Back in the fourth century B.C., Dionysius, the Tyrant of Syracuse, was able to outsmart the discipline of gold and pull his treasury out of a financial jam through the masterful use of monetary policy.

An obscure civil servant of rare ingenuity, Dionysius used the defeat of the Syracusans by the Carthaginians in 406 B.C. as the opportunity to grab power. He denounced the Syracusan generals for their incompetence in letting themselves get beaten and got himself elected Supreme General. He then proceeded to build up the power of Syracuse through a long series of expensive wars. The cost of his armies and fortifications, along with the high cost of government, was heading Syracuse toward bankruptcy. Taxes had reached the level of 20 per cent of each citizen's capital, and additional revenue raised through the looting of temples was insufficient to cover the government's expenses.

His first monetary maneuver was that old ploy, debasing the coinage. He took to adding tin to silver coins and silver to gold coins. It wasn't enough.

Dionysius, presumably after speaking to the despot's equivalent of the Council of Economic Advisers, moved into the realm of sophisticated monetary policy.

He ordered all citizens to turn in their coins but advised them not to worry—they would be paid back. (Those who worried and were caught holding out on the Tyrant were executed.) He restamped the coins, marking them up to double their original worth; paid off the government's debts out of the profit in this little caper and then repaid the citizens dollar for dollar—or ducat for ducat, or whatever the Syracusans were using for money in those days. Thus, with the guile and gall of a modern finance minister, this crafty ruler was able to pay off his creditors and keep his word to the citizenry by the simple expedient of doubling the money supply.

Luckily, in olden days people still believed in poetic justice, and Dionysius got his. A lover of the theater, he entered his original dramas in the Athenian competition year after year and was a consistent loser. Finally, in 367 B.C., one of his plays was awarded first prize. He was so elated that he drank himself to death celebrating his victory.

In our own time, the same crowd that has been pushing for a return to the gold standard and for the right of American citizens to own gold is also pressing for a massive upward revaluation of gold.

These people want $200-an-ounce gold or $1,000-an-ounce gold—the higher the better. It seems the gold-standard types have their own double standard. It's dreadful when those sneaky politicians feed the fires of inflation by grinding out more and more paper money, but to increase the money supply through a huge increase in the price of gold is the only way to get the world back on a sound monetary footing. The difference, of course, is that an increase in the price of gold will profit those who have been hoarding it all these years, while increasing the money supply by printing paper serves only the purposes and profit of the dirty politicians.

Europeans are much more taken with gold than Americans largely because of their experience with devaluations.

Up until 1971, there had been only two formal devaluations of the dollar in terms of gold in our entire history. The price of gold was first established by the U.S. Government at $19.75 an ounce in 1792, It remained there until 1834, when the price was raised to $20.67. The next increase was 100 years later, when President Franklin D. Roosevelt "doubled" the price of gold to $35 an ounce in an effort to reverse the deflation of the depression years.

However, in Europe, currency devaluations were a regular occurrence. France, as the country that was one of the most regular devaluators, is understandably most devoted to gold.

And the high priest of gold is generally conceded to be Jacques Rueff, a French octogenarian who served as President de Gaulle's economic adviser, and who frequently turns up as a speaker where the gold bugs congregate.

At one such meeting in Harriman, New York—sponsored by the Committee for Monetary Research and Education, a group that claims neutrality but seems to invite an inordinate number of pro-gold speakers—M. Rueff proposed a "Marshall Plan for the United States." The proposal was made in March of 1973, when one of the big issues in the international financial field was what to do about the "dollar overhang." This was some $80 billion or so in dollars that were in the hands of foreigners and were no longer convertible into gold.

He called his proposal a method to repay the United States for its generous aid in helping to rebuild Europe after World War II—or as M. Rueff put it: "A concretized expression of the deep gratitude of Western European nations for the generous help they received from the United States under the original Marshall Plan at the end of World War II."

His plan was simple: Raise the official price of gold to $70 an ounce. This would increase the value of the U.S. gold stock to $20 billion from $10 billion. It would also boost the value of the other Western nations' gold stocks to $62 billion from $31 billion. The United States would be offered a 20-

or 25-year loan at a low interest rate, and the money would be used to repay foreign balances to those who wanted cash and restore the dollar's convertibility into gold.

"I am quite certain," said M. Rueff,

that the United States, having at its disposal $41 billion in gold (consisting of $31 billion from the loans I have proposed, plus the $10 billion the Americans will already have from revaluing their own gold holdings) will be able to reduce to a very small amount the balance that has to be repaid. At the same time, enough of this sum will be left to strengthen the U.S. gold reserves materially and thus make possible full convertibility of the dollar.

What would be the cost to France of this generous gesture? By using the dollar and its buying power to raise the value of gold, France would make a nice profit on her official gold holdings, not to mention the Frenchmen who have squirreled away their little bags of Napoleons. Further, the French government would have its gold profit invested in the United States, where it would earn interest, rather than resting shining and sterile with the Bank of France.

The Rueff plan was nothing more than a refinement of the Dionysius swindle of the ancient Greek empire. The major difference was that M. Rueff lacked the persuasive power of Dionysius: the capacity to chop off the head of anyone who declined to accept the generous proposal.

The use of gold as currency is a barter system. Gold is a commodity, and when you buy something for gold you are trading one commodity for another commodity or for a service.

The true believers are convinced that gold has intrinsic value and if the world goes to pot, that value will remain immutable. There is nothing that has intrinsic value under all circumstances, and the only time gold has value is when the community at large is ready to exchange some of its product for gold.

In an affluent society in which food, shelter and the other
basic necessities of life are relatively abundant, gold will
have an attraction both as monetary metal and for decorative
purposes. But get the kind of economic collapse that some
gold hoarders are trying to protect themselves against and
dry bread and sour cheese will fetch more in the market
place than bags of Mexican 50-peso gold pieces.

The link between affluence and a rising price for gold was
analyzed for a gold-bug meeting in the fall of 1973 by David
Lloyd Jacob, an expert in the field. The delegates to the
meeting, held in Montreal and billed as the "International
Monetary Seminar," came to hear about the dreadful inflation that was overtaking the world and how gold was their
only salvation. Jacob indicated that the price of gold was
headed upward—that was what they wanted to hear—but his
reasoning assumed prosperity, not disaster.

He pointed out that the bulk of gold for fabrication is sold
in countries where the per capita income is over $1,000.

"Over the next few years," Jacob said,

the demand for gold is likely to go on rising. Fabrication demand is
closely related to the available cash that people have for leisure and
luxury spending. Relatively little effort has been put into the marketing of gold jewelry, etcetera, and the potential increase in demand in
the advanced countries alone could be enormous. One must, I think,
assume that the less developed countries will continue their advance
towards prosperity and that when they achieve income levels of a
thousand dollars per head, they will more or less conform to the patterns of countries that have already reached the level of prosperity.

In other words, demand for gold goes up with affluence,
and so do gold prices. Would the gold price remain immutable if affluence departs? I doubt it.

The nature of money is difficult to define. The textbooks
define it as a "medium of exchange," but that's a cop-out.
How many kids do you know who've gone through school

and will tell you that money is a "medium of exchange" and not have the haziest idea what they're talking about?

Vaguely, a medium of exchange is a means of exchanging what we have or do for something someone else has or does. In barter, this is done directly. With a monetary system we use an intermediary—money.

In addition to being a medium of exchange, money is supposed to be a store of value and a standard of value. It works pretty well as a standard of value or yardstick to measure relative values. If a pair of shoes costs $30 and a plane trip to Washington costs $30, we know that a pair of shoes is worth an airline ticket to Washington. Money is very helpful if you want to buy a pair of shoes and don't happen to have a plane ticket to exchange for it.

But as a store of value, money has been a failure—a dollar saved today will not be the same dollar next year—and the gold bugs think they have the answer. Paper money depreciates if it is printed faster than the rate at which goods and services are produced. Gold, on the other hand, cannot be created except at the relatively slow pace of 1,370 tons a year, and therefore, say the gold bugs, it will not depreciate. It will hold on to its value no matter what, they say, and they point to the thousands of years of history in which gold has been universally accepted as money.

If gold were truly an immutable store of value, I'd be the first to grab it. But it isn't. Gold is a commodity that has beauty and other admirable qualities, but it doesn't perform miracles. By now we should have learned enough to use a form of money that doesn't restrict economic growth to the rate at which a South African miner can dig dirt out of the ground.

Money is a measure used to keep track of what has gone into and is going out of the economy. When you earn money, society is placing a value on your contribution. You put so much into the economy; therefore you're entitled to take so much out of it. But there must be continuity in society or you're out of luck. The economy that paid you for your input must survive for you to get your share out. If it doesn't, there is nothing paper money or gold can do. And most important, in the aggregate we can take out of the economy only what we put into it, and no amount of fiscal or monetary manipulation can alter this truth.

A dollar is a receipt issued by the Government which certifies that the holder is entitled to take a dollar's worth of goods or services out of the economy.

The government that issued that dollar has the power to tax, which means that it can acquire whatever resources it needs to ensure that the receipt will be honored. Furthermore, the dollar is legal tender and must be accepted by anyone within the jurisdiction of our government in payment for any debts.

This dollar is not convertible into gold but is convertible into a dollar's worth of anything produced in our trillion-dollar-plus economy. In other words, instead of a dollar that says you can bring it to Fort Knox in exchange for 1/35 or 1/42 of an ounce of gold—which I don't want or need—it says this dollar will buy a couple of gallons of gasoline or a belt of cheap booze or a short cab ride or a couple of quarts of milk or a cheeseburger or admission to a third-run movie.

In a discussion about the use of coal as a possible substitute for oil in home heating, a friend asked the rhetorical question "Why dig it up if the environmentalists say it's too dirty and won't let you burn it?"

Gold is dug up, melted into nice yellow bars and then buried again in Fort Knox or the Federal Reserve Bank of New York or a vault in the Bank of England, where it must be guarded day and night at no small expense.

If you don't use it, why dig it up? This seems a reasonable question, but when dealing with gold, reason is not always pertinent.

Over the centuries men have fought, clawed and dug for gold and only a fraction of it has been put to use. Of all the gold mined, about half is in the monetary system of the non-Communist world. The rest has found its way into various private uses such as serving as mattress stuffers for French peasants, teeth for Japanese geisha girls or decorations for the tombs of Egyptian kings.

The monetary use of gold goes back thousands of years, but credit for the first gold coins go to King Croesus of Lydia, whose name has become synonymous with great wealth. He ruled an area that is now western Turkey about 560 years before Christ. Lydia was a principal gold producer of the period, and the first coins were large bean-shaped ingots.

For primitive societies, gold was a great step forward from oxen or axe handles as a medium of exchange. This mysterious metal that never tarnished and shone like the moon had to be a big hit with the kind of society in which you worshiped a fire god and danced around in circles to make it rain and the center of civilization was a temple that looked great with gold decorations.

While we've made tremendous technological progress since the fire-god days—we seed clouds to make it rain and have developed plastic temple decorations—we still cling to gold as money.

The largest single accumulation of the yellow metal anywhere is in the basement of the Federal Reserve Bank of New York. Here about 14,000 tons, worth around $16.5 billion (at $42.22 an ounce) is stacked neatly in bins and guarded with an elaborate security system. Even the president of the bank is not permitted in the vault by himself, and there are guards with submachine guns, and thick fortresslike walls. Most of the gold stored here belongs to foreign governments, and when there is a transfer of ownership between governments, the gold is merely moved from one bin to another.

The bank boasts that depositors have so much faith in the security system that "few have ever asked to examine their gold, even during audits."

This suggests to me that if all the gold were to be quietly stolen and the governments kept unaware of the theft, it would not make a damn bit of difference to anyone. The guards could still stand with their submachine guns, and when orders came to transfer gold from one government to another, the guards could substitute giant Mary Jane candy bars and life would go on.

But the Fed takes its responsibility very seriously and has a scale for weighing the gold that is so sensitive it can detect weights down to 1/100 of a troy ounce, or about one-third the weight of a dollar bill. A troy ounce is 1.097 avoirdupois ounces.

World War II and the huge postwar balance-of-payments deficits in the United States were responsible for the accumulation of gold at the New York Fed. Just prior to and during the war, some $5 billion in gold came from Europe to the United States for safekeeping.

Then in the late 50's and early 60's, as the United States settled its balance-of-payments deficits in gold, another $9 billion accumulated in the basement of the New York Federal Reserve Bank credited to the accounts of foreigners. This was gold formerly owned by the United States but transferred to our foreign creditors without physically leaving the country.

Most of the U.S.-owned gold stock remains outside the Fed's vaults. About half of it is in Fort Knox, Kentucky, and the rest in the Denver and Philadelphia mints and the New York and San Francisco assay offices.

In this century, the diminishing role of gold in our domestic monetary system began with the Great Depression. The problem in the 30's was deflation, particularly in the prices of agricultural products. One of Roosevelt's objectives

in raising the price of gold in 1934 was to get the price of
cotton up to 10 cents a pound, corn up to 50 cents a bushel
and wheat up to 90 cents a bushel. (In 1974 cotton hit a
peak of $1, corn, $3.50, and wheat, $6.50.) It was felt that
devaluing the dollar through raising the price of gold would
make prices rise and agricultural products increase in
price faster than industrial products. The Government also
launched a massive program of commodity purchases.

In 1931 and 1932, gold was flowing out of the country because of payments deficits, and this was reducing the monetary base and aggravating deflation.

Hoarding of gold was further shrinking the money supply
and adding to deflation. In April of 1933, all domestic monetary gold was ordered turned in to the Federal Reserve
Banks. Later that same month, Roosevelt issued orders barring the export of gold. This had the effect of devaluing the
dollar abroad and represented the abandonment by the
United States of a rigid gold standard.

At the time, the major industrial nations were meeting in
London at the World Economic Conference in an effort to
stabilize international currency values. The gold standard,
which Britain had left in 1931, was crumbling, and the international currency market was a kind of free-for-all in which
each country was trying to gain a competitive advantage
over everyone else through manipulating its currency.

The London conference was effectively scuttled by Roosevelt, who sent a message criticizing the conferees for putting
the stabilization of currencies ahead of more pressing problems; ". . . the sound internal economic system of a nation
is a greater factor in its well-being than the price of its currency," the President said.

Joining the game of competitive devaluation, Roosevelt
embarked on the program to raise the gold price. After much
debate over legalities, the President announced on October
22 that the Reconstruction Finance Corporation would buy

gold in the open market at prices set by the President and his advisers. The plan was to gradually increase the gold price and hopefully the price of other commodities.

One day before the announcement of U.S. plans to buy gold, the price on the London market was $29.01 an ounce. On October 25, the first day of trading after the announcement, gold rose to $31.02. By gradual and arbitrary rises in the U.S. buying price, gold reached $35 an ounce in January of 1934. To confuse the speculators, the rate of increase was kept irregular. At one point, the price was increased by 21 cents because Roosevelt considered it a lucky number. "It's three times seven," the President told his advisers.

On January 30, 1934, Congress passed the Gold Reserve Act, and the next day the President set the price of gold at $35 an ounce—reducing the dollar to 59.06 per cent of its pre-1933 gold content, or nearly doubling the price of gold.

To maintain the $35-an-ounce price, the Federal Reserve Bank would sell gold to foreign central banks whenever the price moved above that level. Also, individual Americans could buy gold abroad, but if they had it shipped to the United States they would have to sell it to the Treasury for $35 an ounce.

This created an arbitrage opportunity whenever the foreign price of gold fell far enough below the cost of bringing it into this country, where it could be sold to the Treasury for $35. Furthermore, the Treasury itself could buy foreign gold to support the price, and this was done on a large scale. In February and March of 1934, the Treasury bought a total of $637 million worth, and its heavy purchases soon established the $35-an-ounce price throughout the world. U.S. gold buying continued, however; during 1934 the United States bought $1 billion worth, in 1935 we bought $1.9 billion and in 1936 we added $1.1 billion in gold purchases.

The result of the new gold policy of Roosevelt was to move the United States from a gold standard to a gold-exchange standard. On the surface, the difference between the two systems was that gold no longer circulated freely as currency in the United States, as it had done in the gold-standard days. However, gold remained the ultimate backing for domestic currency and continued to be used to settle up payments deficits between countries.

The fundamental difference between the two systems was that the gold standard had been basically tied to British sterling and the gold-exchange standard was linked to the American dollar.

Economist Sidney Homer, for many years a partner in the investment house of Salomon Brothers, addressed this subject in a talk in January, 1968—a time when there was a frenzied run on gold.

"At no time has any large share of domestic or international payments been made in gold," said Homer,

and at no time has liquid wealth been largely held in gold. Gold has been useful only to the extent that it could always be converted into at least one dominant strong national currency. I believe it can be said that the nineteenth-century world was, in fact, on a sterling standard. The British fortified their sterling standard by maintaining gold convertibility. They were smart enough to call their worldwide sterling standard by the attractive title "gold standard." In this way, the British financial hegemony was sold to the French and many others.

Homer's principal point in that talk was that gold required the support of a strong currency, but at the same time, until there was a supranational government that had the power to declare some form of legal tender, gold would have to play a role in the international monetary system.

Domestically, gold has been gradually phased out of our money system. Under the gold-exchange standard, a gold backing of 40 per cent on all Federal Reserve notes was required, and national-bank deposits were covered by gold reserves of 35 per cent. With the winding down of World War

II and the establishment of a new international money system, the gold backing for Federal Reserve notes was cut to 25 per cent.

In the post–World War II period, as the U.S. economy grew and prospered, gold faded into the monetary background. The dollar became the world's dominant currency, and most nations were just as happy to have dollars in their reserves as gold.

The United States tolerated gold because some foreigners thought it was important. The attitude in official U.S. Government circles was that eventually gold would be demonetized, free to find its own way in commodity markets with platinum, copper, zinc, lead, molybdenum and the rest. The price remained at $35, and there was little interest in the yellow metal in respectable circles. Only a hard core of middle-aged, middle- to upper-class conservatives with their rumpled gray suits and Herbert Hoover collars continued to keep alive the centuries-old mystique. They surfaced with a vengeance when the dollar began to flounder.

In the late 40's, the U.S. gold stock grew to embarrassing proportions, and at one point we had a monetary gold hoard of $24.9 billion, or 70 per cent of the world's monetary gold stock. But then with the Marshall Plan, foreign aid, huge foreign investments by American corporations and a general extravagance, the United States began running up a string of payments deficits that eventually was to undermine confidence in the dollar. In 1963, the official dollar liabilities of the United States crossed the $15 billion mark going up, and the U.S. gold reserve hit $15 billion on the way down.

By 1968, the United States had run up a string of 17 out of 18 years in which our balance of payments was in deficit.

The world was getting nervous about the dollar. Would it be possible for the United States to ever again return to a position of surplus or even of equilibrium? As it turned out, it was not until 1973, after a series of severe crises and two devaluations of the dollar, that a payments surplus was announced. Later the figures were revised and the surplus became a deficit, but in terms of the impact on the dollar, the announcement of a surplus served as well as the reality.

In 1960 there was a flurry of interest in gold and the price in the London market ran up to $40. This prompted the establishment of the London gold pool, in which the United States and seven other financial powers agreed to sell gold at the official price of $35 an ounce whenever demand threatened to push the price materially higher. The plan was similar to the price-stabilization scheme the United States had used in the 30's.

France, which couldn't stomach the loss of its official gold reserves to private hoarders and speculators, quietly withdrew from the pool in mid-1967, leaving the United States, Britain, Belgium, Germany, Italy, the Netherlands and Switzerland to feed the hungry gold bugs. There was no announcement of France's withdrawal, but the fact came out when the British devalued the pound in November, 1967, and there was a concurrent run on gold.

In an effort to shore up the dollar internationally and perhaps save the gold pool, the United States took another step in the process of wiping out the remnants of the gold standard in the domestic money supply. The 25 per cent gold cover on U.S. paper money was removed early in 1968. (The gold cover on bank deposits had been removed in 1965.) The removal of the last vestige of the gold standard domestically had the effect of freeing our entire gold stock—then about $12 billion—for defending the dollar against short-term claims of foreigners that had reached $31 billion. It also meant U.S. currency could be printed without any gold backing.

The removal of the gold cover was ineffective either in restoring confidence in the U.S. dollar or in dampening speculation in gold overseas. The gold pool provided a

unique speculative opportunity: a chance to make money
with almost no downside risk. Seven of the world's major financial powers stood ready to pay all comers $35 an ounce
for gold, providing speculators with a floor under the price.
What could you lose, except a little interest and the commission charges? But if the lid blew, there was no limit to
the profit potential.

As buying pressure from speculators mounted and billions
in official reserves were leaking into private hands—just in
the month of December, 1967, the United States lost nearly
$1 billion in gold reserves—it became clear that the gold pool
would break down. It did.

On March 17, 1968, after an emergency meeting in Washington, the gold-pool nations issued a communiqué which
described the abandonment of the gold pool and the establishment of a two-tier gold market.

One tier provided for the continuation of the $35-an-ounce
official price for dealings among governments and central
banks. The other tier was to be a free market in which private users of gold and speculators could buy and sell at
whatever price supply and demand dictated.

For U.S. citizens, who were shut out of the action in gold
by legal restrictions against owning or dealing in it, the new
system seemed to make little difference. Only those who
used gold commercially and were licensed by the Treasury
were directly affected. Once the two-tier market was set up,
the Treasury no longer sold gold to licensed users here. The
jewelers and the dentists had to go to the free market for
supplies and pay the free-market price.

The split gold market was considered a stopgap, and many
experts were predicting that it would break down in a matter
of weeks or months. However, it proved remarkably stable
and didn't start to collapse until 1971 when the United States
devalued the dollar and suspended convertibility of the dollar into gold. In the formal devaluation, what we did was say

the dollar is now worth only 1/38 of an ounce of gold, instead of 1/35 of an ounce, and furthermore you can't have any even at that price.

President Nixon's "temporary suspension" of the convertibility of the dollar into gold on August 15, 1971, effectively ended the international monetary system that had been set up in 1944 in Bretton Woods, New Hampshire.

Even before the suspension of convertibility, the movement of gold between governments dried up with the end of the London gold pool. As the price of gold on the private tier moved up, the official price became a fiction and the two U.S. devaluations—raising gold in 1971 to $38 an ounce and in February, 1973, to $42.22—did little to restore a reasonable relationship between the official price and the free-market price.

For the first couple of years after the gold pool was disbanded, the free-market price of gold rose only moderately, running $5 an ounce or so above the official price. There was even a point at which the free-market price briefly dipped below the official one. But in 1971 increases in the free market began to accelerate, and by August of 1971 gold was nearing $45 an ounce. The following year, as the international money system traced a crisis-to-crisis pattern, free-market gold soared to $70 an ounce. Another big jump came in 1973 as gold went to $100 an ounce (vs. the $42.22 official price), and in November, 1974, gold topped $180.

Because of the 1933 laws against owning or trading in gold in the United States and a 1961 amendment making it illegal for U.S. citizens to hold gold abroad, potential U.S. speculators were cut off from the fun. The penalty for violation of the Treasury's gold regulations is a fine of up to $10,000, imprisonment for up to ten years or both. This added an extra variable to the risk/reward ratio for gold speculation and kept all but the most rabid gold fans out of the bullion market.

The only avenue open to U.S. gold fetishists was to invest in gold-mining stocks or gold coins. Neither was satisfactory to the purists, because the prices of gold-mining stocks were blown up with at least as much air as gold reserves, and gold coins sold at a premium of 25 per cent or better over the value of their gold content. In other words, if gold was selling at $100 an ounce, a gold coin with an ounce of gold would go for $125 or better. Furthermore, you had to buy gold coins at the retail price and resell them at the wholesale price—another dilution to speculative profits.

This angered the gold bugs, and pressure mounted to permit U.S. citizens to own gold.

The Par Value Modification Act, passed by Congress on September 21, 1973, gave the President the authority to legalize gold ownership for U.S. citizens if he determined that it would not hurt the U.S. balance of payments.

In the summer of 1974 Congress passed and the President signed a bill legalizing gold ownership effective January 1, 1975.

In September of 1971 the National Committee to Legalize Gold had been formed with the goal of initially making it legal for U.S. citizens to own gold and ultimately to repeal the legal-tender laws.

Gold legalization, the committee said, "the logical first step in a rational money reform," should take place immediately.

The second step should be a law allowing gold clauses in contracts. Contracts would be thus guaranteed against loss due to inflation of the fiat dollar. The third step would be the complete repeal of legal tender laws allowing the private mintage of gold coins and the general circulation of private gold money. At this point, there would be a "parallel standard" between gold and the U.S. fiat dollar. The relative use of each money would depend on public trust. If the public found that the value of the fiat dollar was falling in relation to gold, then it is likely gold [would] gradually replace the fiat dollar as the monetary standard in the U.S. Of course, this is a long process, the first step of which is fairly simple: Repeal gold prohibition. We think Americans should ask this question: Why does the U.S. Government maintain that gold is no longer of monetary merit, that it is a "barbarous relic," should be considered in the same way as zinc, lead, copper, or any other metal, and yet maintaining all of this, still refuses to let the people have the choice between the fiat dollar and gold? If U.S. money managers are really confident they can rationally control the supply of fiat dollars, then why should they be afraid of a free gold market?

The committee literature equated gold with freedom and peace and everything nice:

"A free gold market means a free people," the committee declared.

Gold has always been a friend of oppressed people. Totalitarian governments of all types, left and right, have always feared gold. It is the one money not subject to total control. Unlike fiat currency, the supply of gold cannot be arbitrarily inflated to pay for welfare-warfare schemes. Once in the hands of the people gold can be a powerful weapon against statist oppression. Both Hitler and Stalin realized that a free gold market is incompatible with an enslaved people and laws against gold ownership were harshly enforced. They realized a free gold market would have given the people a choice between the state's fiat currency and gold, a choice which would have meant the end of a rigidly controlled monetary system. Gold is an international money accepted without question all over the world. An international money in the hands of the people would have meant escape from foreign exchange controls and perhaps escape from the country. During World War II, persons who had the foresight and opportunity to buy gold were able to flee fascist and communist oppressors with their life savings intact. Those who did not have the opportunity to buy gold had their life savings confiscated or lost everything in worthless government bonds and fiat currency.

Another pro-gold group, the Committee to Reestablish the Gold Standard, wanted to move a little faster than the mere legalization of gold. CRGS contended that merely to legalize gold would benefit the Western mining interests but would have no effect on the nation's economy. What this country really needed, said CRGS, was repeal of the legal-tender laws—step three in the program outlined by NCLG. As long as paper money circulated as legal tender, Gresham's law about bad money's driving out good money would keep legal gold from circulating according to CRGS.

If gold was to help the poor and the average man, it must be through abolition of legal-tender laws and "full restoration of the gold standard," this committee proclaimed.

A chart distributed with the CRGS manifesto showed that every major U.S. war—the War of 1812, the Civil War, World Wars I and II—had coincided with the suspension of the gold standard or a major issue of new paper money. Furthermore, "the period since the abandonment of the gold standard has been a period of continual wars and heavy armaments." The implication of this information is that in some way gold prevents wars and if we just stayed on the gold standard, nations would stop fighting each other. Such is the faith of the true gold bug.

The gold bug is an easily identifiable species. He wears white shirts and narrow ties and gray suits and is so emotionally attached to gold that to even question its status as the only true money will incite instant paroxysm. His mouth will twitch, the veins of his neck will protrude fearfully and his face will turn to a mask of violence. There is a deep attachment to this metal that is like nothing else in this world.

Politically, gold seems to attract the superconservative element—or, as they like to call themselves, libertarians. These are the fellows who generally have lots of money and don't like the idea of any government's taking it away from them through such radical notions as progressive taxation. They are strong believers in the free market as the only way to run an economy, and the misallocation of resources resulting from such programs as social security or free milk for babies is not to be tolerated. The only restrictions they are willing to accept are those imposed by the law of supply and demand and the discipline of gold.

In keeping with a conservative philosophy, the gold glori-
fiers are deeply suspicious of plans for international economic cooperation. What they hope to do with a gold standard is duck the real issue in any international monetary
system—national sovereignty. They hope gold can place the
kind of discipline on each nation that will force it to conform
with the gold bug's idea of monetary responsibility. Unfortunately, history has shown that when national interests conflict with international interests, each nation will try to save
its own economy, and gold can be manipulated to this end
as readily as paper money.

Inflation, in the eyes of the gold bug, is a socialist plot to
redistribute resources, since the working classes can get constant pay raises while the middle and upper classes, who live
on savings and investments, find that inflation is robbing
them of their accumulated wealth.

Milton Friedman, as conservative and free-marketish a
fellow you'd ever want to meet, is not pure enough for the
gold bugs. While Friedman thinks the government should
legalize gold ownership here and keep its cotton-picking
hands off the economy, his economics has one fatal flaw. He
believes that the government should control the money supply and keep it growing at a constant rate. This is unpalata-
ble for the back-to-the-gold-standard types, who would have
the South African miners determine whether or not our
money supply grows.

While there is much emotional zeal among gold boosters,
there are also some strong emotions on the other side. The
anti-gold forces feel that gold should never be restored to an
important place in the international monetary system because to do so would reward the speculators—those dirty
dogs who bet against the dollar. Restoring gold to importance would also benefit South Africa, whose major claim to
fame, aside from gold and diamonds, is its devotion to apart-
heid and white supremacy.

The posture of South Africa makes it comfortable for most

conservatives to espouse the rethroning of gold, but it would require some schizophrenic reasoning for a liberal to press for reinstitution of the gold standard.

The Soviet Union is another potential beneficiary of any upgrading of the status of gold in the monetary system, since Russia is probably the world's second-largest gold producer. This should make the 100 per cent American conservative gold bug a bit uneasy; when there is a clash between money and ideology, we tend to put first things first—money.

Harry D. Schultz, Ph.D., D.Sc., an American who works out of London, is one of the established leaders of the gold sect, and every year he runs a rally for the faithful billed as an "International Monetary Seminar." He brings together gold apologists from around the world, and they have a fine time tearing apart politicians who have debased the world's currencies with their printing-press money. The seminars are well attended, and Dr. Schultz reportedly makes great gobs of paper money as the sponsor.

The essence of the gold bug's arguments and the emotional overtones can be garnered from the following, quoted from one of the speakers at a Harry Schultz seminar:

Everything that has happened to the U.S. dollar since 1933 has been the result of a deliberate iniquitous and continuous conspiracy to downgrade gold, and ultimately demonetize it, and to pave the way for monetarily illiterate and devious politicians to perpetuate the errors of Keynes, through progressive inflation, ever rising costs of labor, escalating debts and printing of paper dollars without limit—all in a hopeless endeavor to maintain full employment and escape recession or depression. The premise of two generations of dead politicians in America that gold is outmoded has been dead wrong. The cumulative financial wisdom of intelligent men for 2600 years clearly established gold as the ideal and the essential monetary metal for any nation destined for greatness and survival.

Gold is glorified as having a power that just cannot be matched by mere man. Listen to this tribute to the "king of metals" excerpted from a talk at another gold-bug convention:

Almost all commodities you can name wear out, break up, are consumed or become eroded, rusted, tarnished, used up or thrown away. Except gold! Gold because of its unique qualities is different. It is the most beautiful of metals with a permanent yellow luster that has attracted men and enraptured women since its magnetic glitter in dust or nuggets first caught the attention of the river people along the banks of the Nile and the Euphrates, thousands of years ago. Gold is malleable, ductile, ornamental, divisible, is easily alloyed or worked with other metals, heat resistant and an excellent conductor of electricity . . .

Citing the 6,000-year-history of gold, the speaker said that "only a jackass" would say gold was a "barbarous relic." As I say, these people get very uptight about anyone who tries to knock gold.

Another group strongly in favor of a return to gold as the core of the monetary system naturally enough represents the gold-mining interests. Donald H. McLaughlin, chairman of the executive committee of the Homestake Mining Company, the largest U.S. gold producer, says that a return to the gold standard is critical to restoring economic health to the United States and its trading partners.

At a symposium on gold in San Francisco in April of 1974, Mr. McLaughlin said that if a new international monetary system were to have any "prospect of permanence" it would have to be based on gold.

Another speaker raised the prospect that the Arabs would demand gold for their oil and force the world back onto a gold standard.

My own feeling is that the gold standard could be a weapon to get back at the Arabs for cutting off our oil supplies in the fall of 1973. We could raise the official price of gold to $500 an ounce and overnight increase our $11 billion gold stock to $120 billion. We could then exchange this overpriced gold for oil, and by the time the gold stock was exhausted (if it starts to run out too quickly, we'll just revalue it again) we'd be converted to atomic or solar power. The

Arabs could then line their empty oil wells with gold and maybe sell tickets to tourists.

The idea of a sharply higher official price of gold appears to be the driving force behind the speculative run on the metal since the 1971 dollar devaluation. The speculators reason that without the dollar as an anchor for the monetary system, gold will have to take its place. There is also the matter of the $80 billion or so in foreign claims against the dollar that many believe can be repaid only through a Dionysius-like maneuver involving a massive increase in the official gold price.

The United States has been staunchly opposed to this type of solution for repayment of its overseas debts; but it was just as strongly against dollar devaluation prior to August 15, 1971. Such a devaluation was regarded as unthinkable—but circumstances have a way of overruling philosophical principles.

Behind the laudatory speeches about the virtues of gold lurks the hope that the price will be pushed way up. Gold at $1,000 an ounce would be the first step to Paradise.

What the $1,000-gold advocates are rooting for is inflation under gold rather than inflation under paper money. Paul A. Volcker, former Under Secretary of the Treasury for Monetary Affairs and a leading expert in the field, in an interview with *Investing* magazine put it this way:

> The discipline of gold works only if nobody changes the price. Once you admit that the same men who print money will in effect "print" the price of gold, all you've done is to find a new way of printing paper money.

There was a period after World War II when the U.S. dollar was so strong that if we had wanted to demonetize gold we probably could have accomplished it. But after a couple of decades of spending more abroad than we earned, that opportunity has slipped away. While a hoard of gold, whatever its nominal value, is no match for a trillion-dollar-plus economy, modern man has not become so rational a being that he doesn't need a voodoo symbol to make him feel secure.

Gold is that symbol. Just as a security blanket will not really protect a child from the demons that might invade his room at night, it works fine as long as there are no real demons.

Gold makes the insecure feel that they are being protected from the demons of runaway inflation and a collapsing economy. But let the economy be plunged into a major depression or postinflation collapse and gold will prove as effective as the wet end of a tattered piece of wool.

Investment in gold is totally unproductive. Its potential for profit rests on the "greater fool" theory so popular during the boom days of the 1967–68 stock market. In those days, a fool bought a stock selling at 50 times earnings and could make money if he found a greater fool who would pay 60 times earnings. So it is with gold. One fool pays $150 an ounce for gold and can make money as long as he can find someone willing to pay $160 an ounce for it. The buyer must then find someone willing to pay $170, and so on. While the supply of fools may appear inexhaustible, their number is finite, and ultimately the last fool is left holding the gold.

It reminds me of the story of the imported sardines. A dealer bought a boatload of sardines from Norway for 10 cents a can and quickly sold them to another dealer for 12 cents a can, who sold them to a third dealer for 15 cents a can. The third dealer got hungry one day and opened a can of the sardines to eat. They were dreadful, and he quickly got on the phone with his supplier screaming about the poor quality of the sardines.

"You ate them?" said the supplier incredulously. "Those sardines aren't for eating. They're for buying and selling and buying and selling and buying and selling."

So it is with gold. It's for buying and selling and buying and selling and has no other purpose.

There is a clear danger that gold speculators will get badly burned if gold is finally demonetized. The increase in the price in free-market trading has been on a relatively slim volume. Economist Sidney E. Rolfe, writing in *The New York Times* in May of 1974, stated that only about $25 million worth of gold is traded daily in the free market. The holdings of central banks at the free-market price would be worth between $160 and $180 billion. "A relatively small sale of this vast hoard by some central banks could swamp the free market and crack the price."

Getting rid of gold is no easy task. Back in January of 1968 when the world was groping for ways out of a raging gold-buying panic, Dr. Frank C. Genovese, then associate dean of the Graduate School of Babson Institute, suggested that the United States should just unload all its gold on the rest of the world.

Writing in a newsletter distributed by Goodbody & Company, Dr. Genovese outlined a complex plan for getting the U.S. international monetary position back on a sound basis. Part of the plan was to get rid of the "barbarous relic."

"It is a relic of times of poor communication, economic illiteracy, statistical ignorance, and rapacious princes," wrote Dr. Genovese.

A modern world should not need gold. It is a useless form of wealth. Gold should be the world's hot potato. Each country should seek to unload it on other nations so that it can get something useful for it. We should let France and other nations have our gold while we purchase foreign deposits, securities, land, etc. We should seek to convert gold to earning assets or jewelry or fillings for teeth, etc. We presently have an historic opportunity to do just this. Let us continue to unload gold and let us never be so foolish as to try to reacquire it by trading American-owned assets for it.

In all honor, we should state this as our position and let those who want it, acquire gold. As the light of the consequences of this practice

in terms of real assets and inflation dawns on other nations, gold buying will tend to dry up and its use as a monetary base be forsaken.
The relic will be abandoned.

At about the same time, in a much less scholarly tone, I
suggested in a column in the Fairchild newspapers that we
sell our gold and go on a chicken-fat standard, since chicken
fat had the nice yellow color of gold and had the advantage
of being edible.

Well, Goodbody is no longer with us, having gone broke
during the 1969–70 stock-market debacle; chicken fat is used
as a standard of value only among an obscure sect of people
in the Williamsburg section of Brooklyn and the barbarous
relic was going for $180 an ounce the last time I looked.

Guido Hanselmann, a long-time executive of the Union
Bank of Switzerland, the largest of the Swiss banks, revived
a cliché used to explain in simple terms why gold hangs on.

"In a strictly economic sense," he told a meeting of the
New York Society of Financial Analysts in May of 1974,

it is absurd to dig gold out from deep below the ground and then lock
it up underground again in vaults. But if there are three hundred economists who are against gold, there are about three billion inhabitants of
the world who believe in gold. The problem is for the three hundred
economists to convince the three billion others.

III

THE FEDERAL RESERVE SYSTEM

RUNNING THE PRINTING PRESSES IN A BROOKS BROTHERS SUIT

Ambiguity abounds in the world of money and banking. When I first started covering the field, I found that financial types were forever talking about "fiscal policy" and "monetary policy." Having a rudimentary knowledge of the English language, I knew that "fiscal" meant something relating to money and "monetary" obviously related to money. My problem was figuring out the difference between the two.

I was afraid just to ask somebody, because if word got out, who would ever have faith in a financial editor who didn't know his fiscal from his monetary? After listening to dozens of speeches and carefully checking the context in which each term was used, I finally figured out which policy was which. I then did some discreet questioning and was able to confirm my conclusions. Fiscal policy deals with budgetary matters—taxes, government expenditures, deficits and surpluses. The course of fiscal policy is determined by the Federal Administration and Congress. Monetary policy deals with the money supply and interest rates and is the province of the Federal Reserve Board.

Another example of the imprecision of the language of finance is something called Reserves for Private Deposits, or RPD. This is a concept used by the Federal Reserve people as they go about their business of executing monetary policy, and it refers to reserves required to support private nonbank deposits. This really threw me. What the hell were "private nonbank deposits"? I figured they must be deposits in nonbanks. Perhaps deposits made with landlords on leases or deposits at the bottom of old wine bottles. Why would anybody want to make deposits in nonbanks anyhow?

Diligent research turned up the answer: nonbank deposits are bank deposits made by anyone who is not a bank. The "private" referred to nongovernmental deposits. In other words, RPD meant reserves needed to support bank deposits (not nonbank deposits) after subtracting reserves required for U.S. Government and interbank deposits.

And even the word "bank" is ambiguous. There are banks and there are banks, and there are banks that aren't banks at all.

Investment banks aren't banks. In the aftermath of the stock-market crash of 1929, commercial banking and investment banking were separated. Investment bankers are underwriters, stockbrokers, commission merchants, financial advisers and corporate marriage brokers. They don't take deposits and they don't usually make loans.

They try to bring together borrowers and lenders or investors and investees. If they like a deal, they'll guarantee that they can raise the money for it through underwriting stock or bond issues, and if they can't sell the issue they have to eat it. But banking, no.

There are savings banks and savings-and-loan associations which take in deposits and lend the money out primarily on mortgages, but they can't do what real banks—that is, what commercial banks—can do. Commercial banks can create money that never existed and wipe out money with a jab on the computer button. It's done through the magic of the double-entry bookkeeping system and the connivance, if not outright participation, of the Federal Reserve System.

When a commercial bank makes a loan, it creates a deposit on its books against which the borrower can draw. Thus if a customer borrows $100, the bank enters $100 as a deposit on the liability side of its ledgers and $100 as a loan receivable on the asset side. When the money is drawn out, the bank's cash declines by the amount of the withdrawal on the asset side and the deposit declines on the liability side, keeping everything in balance. (In practice, banks do not permit the withdrawal of the full amount of a loan, but require the borrower to keep about 20 per cent of the loan on deposit. This adds to the borrower's effective cost.)

When the loan falls due and the bank gets paid off by a $100 deposit, the loan is wiped off the books and so is the deposit. Thus the money that was created by the original loan has served its purpose and disappears when the loan is repaid.

Although the nation's 14,000 commercial banks have this unique power to create money, they can't do it promiscuously. There are state and Federal regulations about how much a bank can lend, and there's the strong hand of the Federal Reserve System on the money spigot, with the power to let the money gush, drip or just flow out smoothly. In short, the Federal Reserve is the real powerhouse in the money-creating game.

The Federal Reserve System of the United States was established in 1913 as a central bank, and the constitutional power of Congress to coin money and regulate its value was delegated to the Fed.

It is literally a huge money factory, organized along regional lines under the over-all policy leadership of the seven-member Federal Reserve Board of Governors. Board members and the chairman are appointed by the President for fourteen-year terms, subject to Senate approval. There are twelve regional banks located in major financial centers— New York, Chicago, Boston, Philadelphia, San Francisco, Atlanta, Cleveland, Dallas, Kansas City, Minneapolis, Richmond and St. Louis.

So abstruse are the monetary machinations of the Fed that Congressman Wright Patman, Chairman of the House Banking Committee, has referred to the banking system as a plot designed to hoodwink the American public. He called for the news media to blow away the "smoke screen of complexity behind which banks and bank regulators hide their anticonsumer interests."

Instead of merely printing money the way the Germans did in the 1920's, the Fed goes through an obscenely complicated series of bookkeeping entries—moving numbers around, buying and selling Government securities, making loans, buying securities and agreeing to sell them right back, selling securities and agreeing to buy them right back, raising and lowering reserve requirements and discount rates; but when all this activity is analyzed, the Federal Reserve System is creating money out of thin air.

When a Federal Reserve Bank pays the salary of one of its guards, it pays with money it creates. When it buys $250 million worth of Treasury bills, it creates the money to pay for them. And the money the Fed creates has the ability to multiply itself. The experts tell me that $1 added to reserves on deposit with the Fed will eventually grow to $7.80. How this multiplication comes about is linked to those bookkeeping entries which we will explore later. Physical cash means nothing to the Fed, and it can and does burn it at will. Out in San Francisco, the Federal Reserve Bank was accused of polluting the atmosphere by burning old Federal Reserve notes.

The ability of the Fed to manufacture new money is attested to by the fact that in 1930 there was about $4 billion in currency in circulation. By 1974, greenbacks outstanding had grown to $66 billion.

The difference between the German method of the 1920's and the infinitely more sophisticated techniques of the Federal Reserve System is one of form rather than substance. The mechanics for a runaway inflation are readily available here if the Fed chooses to throw open the spigot and let the money gush out. It has not chosen to do so and has acted responsibly in performing an extremely difficult task: supplying the money needed to keep the economy running smoothly.

With the ability to create money, the Federal Reserve System itself turns a nice profit. In 1973, the system earned more than $5 billion and after expenses came in with a net profit of $4,522,000,000. This was almost as much as the combined after-tax income that year of all the commercial banks in the system ($5,012,000,000).

The stock in the Federal Reserve Banks is owned by member banks, but almost all the Fed's profits are turned over to the Treasury. In 1973, about $4.3 billion of the profits went to the Treasury, a piddling $49 million went to member banks as dividends on their stockholdings and another $51 million was kept to finance future operations. With the Fed's ability to create money, there really isn't much need to add to capital, but the system makes a strong effort to look just like any other commercial venture.

It may appear to be grossly unfair for the Federal Reserve to pay over so much of its profits to the Government and so little to its stockholders, but again, this is no ordinary business. The Fed earns most of its money from interest on Government obligations, so the turnover of profits is essentially returning this interest to the Treasury. It's all in the family.

The Fed is not operated for a profit. It is an instrumentality of the Government designed to manage the nation's money supply. The vehicle for getting the money into the hands of the people who will spend it or save it or invest it is the commercial banking system.

The system is so complex that many bank loan officers don't understand it. Fortunately, they don't have to. All they have to know is how to analyze a credit risk. The quality of the loans they make will to a large extent determine the quality of our money supply. A productive loan will inject something of value into our economy, giving the newly created money value.

A businessman borrowing to buy steel to build a refrigerator will add something to the economy provided he has the productive capacity to build it.

On an individual loan basis, the Fed must depend on the banks. But in the aggregate, the monetary authorities must decide if the economy has the capacity to absorb money for greater production or if the money will just dilute the supply. The creation of more money when production can't be increased merely raises prices.

Banks serve as collectors of savings used to create more money and more savings. For capital to form, part of current income must be saved and plowed back into income-generating investments. Banks serve to convert savings into income-producing investments. At least, that's what the bankers say.

There are a narrow money supply, a broad money supply and an in-between money supply. The narrow definition of money is called M_1. This encompasses coin and currency outstanding and demand deposits at commercial banks. In mid-1974 this came to around $280 billion, including about $66 billion in currency. Some contend that this is the only definition of real money, since checks or cash can be readily spent. Savings deposits must first be converted into currency or placed in checking accounts before they can be used for payment.

The intermediate definition of the money supply, M_2,

which stood at $593 billion, takes in currency, checking accounts and time deposits at commercial banks, but excludes large certificates of deposit. These large CD's are considered investments rather than deposits, although it's difficult to see any substantial difference between the CD's and other time deposits. One expert says these large CD's have a tendency to grow rapidly or dry up suddenly, depending on money-market conditions, and would tend to make the monetary aggregates "jump around too much."

In any event, even the broadest definition of the money supply, M_3, did not include the $82 billion in large CD's outstanding. M_3, which stood at $925 billion in mid-1974, is the total of M_2 plus deposits in savings banks and savings-and-loan associations.

There is no reason why the big M classifications can't be stretched out indefinitely to include everything that can be converted into money—from Treasury bills to used cars—but mercifully, most monetarists stop at M_3.

M_1 is the cleanest, if not the best, measure of the money supply, and that's normally what we're dealing with when referring to the money stock.

The role of gold in our domestic money supply is now merely ceremonial, although gold certificates appear prominently as an $11,460,000,000 asset item on the balance sheet of the Federal Reserve System. This represents nearly the entire gold stock of the U.S. Treasury; there is another $200 million in unmonetized Treasury gold that is a holdover from the days when gold was used to back our money and to settle international debts.

The gold certificates are used as collateral for Federal Reserve notes issued, but there's no provision for noteholders to attach the collateral. Over the years, when the Treasury needed money, it would issue gold certificates to the Fed and would be credited with a cash deposit.

Since March 19, 1968, there has been no requirement for

gold backing of Federal Reserve notes, which now account for virtually all the currency in circulation. Nevertheless, the Fed still goes through the motions. Gold certificates, Special Drawing Rights and U.S. Government securities serve as collateral for currency the bank issues. Also, debts among the twelve Reserve Banks are settled through charges and credits against the gold-certificate account of each bank. This shifts gold-certificate balances within the system, but the total remains the same.

There is an *Alice in Wonderland* quality to the bookkeeping entries and balance-sheet items of the Reserve Banks. Federal Reserve notes (cash) show up as a liability. Government bonds, which are obligations of the Government, become assets used for collateral for the Federal Reserve notes, which can be used to buy Government obligations. Since the Treasury and the Reserve System are just two parts of the same government, what's really happening is a lot of switching of paper from one pocket to the other.

However, banks will be banks, so the Fed dutifully lists about $109 billion in assets (as of July 10, 1974) and liabilities of $107 billion. The largest asset item is an $80.7 billion portfolio of U.S. Government securities. It's all frightfully incestuous, but it gets the job done.

Federal Reserve notes are freely circulated and accepted, as are checks which represent claims against commercial banks. About 75 per cent of payments made in the U.S. economy are by check, and money in the bank is as good as—well, as good as money in the bank.

Computer entries are playing an ever-increasing role in the transfer of funds. The New York Federal Reserve Bank now has a computer network that moves about $5 trillion a year. It links twelve large New York City banks with the Federal Reserve System complex. A participating bank can transfer balances instantaneously to any other participating bank.

Money is created when the Fed creates reserves and the banking system makes loans supported by these reserves. The central bank controls the amount of money available by raising and lowering reserves or reserve requirements.

Its basic responsibility is to administer policy so as to balance the supply of money and credit with the needs of the economy. It also attempts to maintain a noninflationary, fully employed growing economy (I said *attempts* to maintain) and watch over our international trade and financial dealings. In addition to the money-supply function, the system supervises and regulates the commercial banking system; handles the mechanics of clearing checks; serves as the fiscal agent for the Federal Government and Federal agencies; handles foreign-exchange and gold transactions and holds gold in its vaults for foreign monetary authorities.

The Federal Reserve Bank of New York handles all foreign-currency operations for the Treasury and intervenes in exchange markets to keep the dollar floating at proper levels. (See Chaos with a College Education.)

But the most important of the Fed's responsibilities is the money supply. It's also the most difficult, since there is no universally acceptable definition of "money supply"—or even of "money," for that matter.

There are major areas of disagreement about the economic impact of changes in the money supply, and there are monumental technical difficulties.

The key to controlling the money supply is the control of bank reserves. The Federal Reserve Board has the right to fix reserve requirements of member banks within a certain range.

At this writing, requirements were fixed at 8 per cent of the first $2 million of demand deposits; 10½ per cent between $2 million and $10 million; 12½ per cent between $10 million and $100 million; 13½ per cent between $100 million and $400 million and 18 per cent over $400 million. On savings deposits, 3 per cent was required up to $5 million and 5 per cent over $5 million.

Originally, the purpose of reserves was simply prudent banking. If a bank went out and made loans without keeping a few dollars in the vault to pay off withdrawals against the deposits it was creating, it could go broke. With a constant flow of money in and out and with loans being made and paid off, the mathematics of a fractional reserve requirement against deposits made it possible to expand the money supply by $7 or $8 or whatever through a $1 increase in reserves.

The amount of reserve dollars in the banking system is the result of decisions by the Federal Reserve System. The Fed can create new reserves by loans to member banks through what is known as the discount window (actually most of these loans are made by computer) and through buying Government securities in its open-market operations. It can also create excess reserves simply by lowering the reserve requirements.

Fooling with reserve requirements is a heavy-handed approach to managing the money supply, and the Fed uses it sparingly. From 1963 to 1974 there had been only four across-the-board changes. With the multiplier effect of changes in reserves, a fractional change in requirements can make massive changes in the money supply.

Another tool the Fed has for affecting the money supply is the discount rate. This is the charge the central bank makes on loans to member banks. The loans are credited directly to a bank's reserve account, creating high-powered money. When the discount rate is low, this will encourage banks to borrow, while high rates will have the opposite effect. This is the logic—but the discount rate in recent years has lagged the money market rather than led it and has been more a symbol of the Fed's attitude than an instrument for changing reserve levels.

The Fed regards discount loans as a privilege member

banks should not abuse. These loans are made to banks for short periods of time (generally 15 days or less) to help a bank with a temporary shortage of reserves. A bank that shows up at the discount window too often is likely to get a phone call from a Federal Reserve official saying, in effect: "Watch it, buddy. You're overdoing a good thing and we're not at all happy with you."

Since the Fed carries immense power and prestige within the banking system, when it speaks bankers listen carefully.

The reluctance of bankers to borrow at the discount window, even when the rate was well below what banks were paying for their money elsewhere, was clearly illustrated in 1974 when the banks were paying out 12 per cent or more on certificates of deposit and the discount rate was only 8 per cent.

It is customary for banks to borrow from one another when some have excess reserves and others are short. Such loans of Federal funds are typically made for overnight or a day or two. The interest rate on Federal funds is the premier indicator of posture of the Federal Reserve on monetary policy. During the money squeeze of 1974, banks were routinely paying 13 or 14 per cent for Fed funds and sometimes as much as 25 to 30 per cent, rather than go to the discount window, where the going rate was 8 per cent.

The really wild Fed-funds quotations generally came on Wednesday afternoons when banks were due to report their level of reserves to the authorities. The penalty for reserve deficiency is a charge of 2 percentage points over the discount rate on the amount of the shortfall. Thus, even the penalty, 10 per cent, was lower than the cost of money elsewhere. Yet banks scrambled to get their reserves to shape up. Such is the awesome power of the Federal Reserve System.

The discount window is also used to handle emergency situations such as the Penn Central failure in 1970, when there was a scare in the money markets and the Fed had to pump reserves into the banking system to prevent a domino pattern of failures. Similarly, in 1974 when the Franklin National Bank in New York got into a jam and there was a runoff of deposits, the Federal Reserve lent the bank over $1 billion to hold it together until a permanent solution could be worked out. Again, the Fed acted to block a collapse of confidence and a possible chain reaction of failures that might follow the massive defaults of what was then the twentieth-largest bank in the country.

Discount loans generally are collateralized by U.S. Government securities, but the Fed has the authority to accept anything it deems satisfactory. This could range from a bank's real estate to the bank president's Louis XIV desk. This type of loan would carry a rate of interest at least ½ point above the discount rate and could run for as long as four months.

The Fed, as the lender of last resort, has authority to make collateralized loans to individuals or partnerships or corporations, but this power is not exercised except under extreme conditions.

In dealing with the money supply on a day-to-day basis, the Federal Reserve System focuses on open-market operations. If the Fed wants to loosen up on money, it goes into the market and buys Government obligations. The money it pays for these securities works its way into the reserves of the banking system. If the money supply needs tightening, it sells Government securities, and the money it gets on these sales is withdrawn from bank reserves.

This is how the Fed attempts to fine-tune the money supply and keep interest rates at levels consistent with policy goals.

The actual buying and selling is done on behalf of the system by the Federal Reserve Bank of New York, since the money markets are located in New York. Policy is mapped out by the Federal Open Market Committee, which meets monthly in Washington to review economic conditions and prepare instructions for the manager of the New York Fed's open-market trading desks.

The committee (FOMC) is made up of the seven members of the Board of Governors; the president of the Federal Reserve Bank of New York, who is a permanent member and serves as vice-chairman, and the presidents of four other Federal Reserve Banks, who serve one-year terms, rotating with the heads of the other Reserve Banks.

The Chairman of the Federal Reserve Board presides over the FOMC, and presidents of Reserve Banks who are not voting members of the committee regularly attend the meetings and take part in the discussion.

When deciding on its domestic monetary policy, the FOMC must also keep an eye on foreign developments, since interest rates have a strong influence on the flow of money internationally. If the FOMC decides that domestic conditions require an expansion of the money supply and lower interest rates, the dollar could be weakened by an outflow of dollars abroad where interest rates are higher. Conversely, if interest rates are higher here than in other major industrial countries, money will be attracted to the United States, bolstering the international value of the dollar.

Out of these meetings will come a broad directive, and the New York manager will implement the policy.

The New York Fed works with a stable of about two dozen "reporting dealers" who make markets in U.S. Government securities. The list changes from time to time as some dealers leave the business and others enter, but the core remains fairly stable. Doing business with the Fed is pretty comfortable. While the profits are small in relation to the numbers (the dealer's spread between what he buys a U.S. security for and what he sells it for is about $75 per $1 million in face value), there's not too much risk when your customer is the Federal Reserve System.

As of March of 1974, the dealers privileged to buy from

and sell to the Fed were Bank of America; Bankers Trust Company; A. G. Becker & Company; Briggs, Schaedle & Company; Chase Manhattan Bank; Chemical Bank; Continental Illinois National Bank & Trust Company of Chicago; Discount Corporation of New York; Donaldson, Lufkin & Jenrette Securities Corporation; First Boston Corporation; First National Bank of Chicago; First National City Bank; First Pennco Securities; Harris Trust and Savings Bank; Aubrey G. Lanston & Company; Merrill Lynch Government Securities; Morgan Guaranty Trust Company of New York; New York Hanseatic Corporation; Northern Trust Company; John Nuveen & Company; Wm. E. Pollock & Company; Chas. E. Quincey & Company; Salomon Brothers; Second District Securities Company and United California Bank.

When the open-market desk wants to buy or sell securities, it canvasses the dealer, gets prices and decides what to take from whom.

The mechanics of a Fed purchase of $250 million worth of Treasury bills from a group of dealers works like this:

The Fed pays the dealers, who deposit the checks in their banks. These banks get credit on their reserve accounts for the amount of the payment. The reserves are dispersed further through the banking system as the dealers repay loans. Nonbank dealers usually borrow around 95 per cent of the value of these securities, so when the Fed pays them, they pay off their creditors—insurance companies, pension funds and other cash-rich financial institutions.

If the dealer is a bank, the Fed credits the bank's reserve account directly.

If the Fed wants to contract bank reserves, it sells securities and puts the money into fiscal quarantine. Reserves are swallowed up.

To counter short-term swings in the money markets, the Fed employs repurchase agreements (repos) or reverse repos. Under a purchase agreement, the Fed buys securities from a dealer who agrees to buy it back within a short period, usually a few days, at the same price. The reverse repos, as we might expect, run the other way. The Fed sells and agrees to repurchase. These transactions are more in the nature of secured loans than sales. That is, in a repo transaction the Fed advances money and takes the securities as collateral, and in reverse, the dealers are lending the Fed money and taking securities as collateral.

In any case, the repos and reverse repos nudge reserves in the direction the Fed wants them to move when the market becomes slightly unbalanced. The Federal funds rate tells the open-market operators what's happening to bank reserves. When the banking system is awash with reserves, the Fed funds rate is low, and as reserves tighten, the Fed funds rate rises.

While all this buying and selling and lending and borrowing is the most important control mechanism for influencing the money supply, it appears to me that the Fed is going through a lot of movement for nothing. The purpose of all this activity is to get bank reserves at the desired level to supply the money needed to mesh with economic conditions and carry out monetary policy. It is conceded that the Fed doesn't know precisely what will happen to reserves from these open-market transactions, although it has a pretty good idea. It is further conceded that the authorities have even less knowledge about how the changes in reserves will translate into changes in the money supply.

I think it would be considerably more precise and infinitely cheaper if the Fed just got up every morning and said: "Today bank reserves are up .0075946 per cent," or "Today bank reserves are down by .0059724 per cent," or whatever the number is that the computer tells them they require to carry out policy. Why do we need all this foolishness to give us a number that is arrived at by a conscious decision rather than by any real market factors?

The only ones to suffer from such a change would be the Government-securities dealers who have been getting this free ride to the money factory.

With so many opportunities for monetary policy to go astray, it would seem reasonable to expect that the Federal Reserve System would have control over all the banks in the country. Surprisingly (at least, it surprised me), in 1973 only 41 per cent of the commercial banks in the United States were members of the system and subject to the Fed's reserve requirements, and the percentage was declining. While member banks controlled 78 per cent of total bank deposits, this figure had also dropped, from 86 per cent in 1947, and was still falling.

How do you control the money supply when more than half the banks are out of your jurisdiction? With great difficulty, that's how.

The reason for the erosion of memberships can be traced to the dual banking system in the United States which permits nationally chartered and state-chartered banks to exist side by side. Bankers, particularly state-chartered bankers, equate dual banking with the Bill of Rights, God, motherhood, liberty and all that is great about America. It permits state banks to operate under the friendly eyes of state legislatures and down-home supervisors rather than submit to cold disciplines emanating from Washington. National banks must be members of the Federal Reserve System. State-chartered banks may choose to become members or to operate outside the system. More and more state banks have opted for nonmembership for the most basic of all business reasons: they can make more money out of it than in it.

Edward G. Boehne, senior vice-president of the Federal Reserve Bank in Philadelphia, pointed out in the June, 1974, edition of the bank's business review that there had been a steady leakage of Fed membership over the past 25 years and the trend was continuing.

To become a member of the Federal Reserve System a bank must agree to buy stock in the system equal to 6 per cent of the member bank's capital. Of this, 3 per cent must be purchased outright and the other 3 per cent is subject to a call from the central bank. The Fed has never called for the extra 3 per cent. Member banks get a dividend payment of 6 per cent of the par value of the stock—not exactly a princely return by recent interest-rate standards. Member banks' reserves must be kept on deposit with the Fed or in the form of currency and coin (it wasn't until November 24, 1960, that member banks were able to count their vault cash as reserves).

Reserves, as far as member banks are concerned, are idle assets that aren't earning any return. While some states set the same reserve requirements as the Federal Reserve (Arkansas, Missouri, Nevada, New Jersey, Utah and Washington), most states are more liberal. Even in the case of nonmember banks, subject to the same reserve requirements as members, there is an advantage. Nonmembers can keep their reserves in demand deposits with other banks, and while they won't earn interest on the money, the depository banks will find other means of expressing their gratitude. This could take the form of lavish entertainment at conventions or free investment-advisory services or referrals of business.

Some states permit their banks to count as reserves interest-bearing U.S. or state securities, or time deposits in other banks. Illinois doesn't require any reserves at all for its state-chartered banks. Kentucky requires reserves representing only 7 per cent of deposits, and 25 per cent of these reserves can be in U.S. securities, Kentucky securities or certificates of deposit from other banks. The higher interest rates go, the more attractive it becomes for banks to leave the system.

Boehne's article also points out that the present setup increases the danger of pyramiding reserves. Under a 10 per cent reserve requirement, a $100 increase in reserves at the Fed could support $1,000 in deposits at member banks, which in turn could support $10,000 in deposits at nonmember banks. This could be further pyramided for the $10,000 to support $100,000, according to Boehne.

If a pending bill proposed by the Fed to standardize reserve requirements for all but the smallest banks is enacted, the monetary authorities would gain control over 97 per cent of the nation's demand deposits. (The Bank of England requires all banks to adhere to the same reserve standards and pays interest on reserves.)

Even if the bill is passed, the Fed would not have perfect control over the money supply. It never knows for sure what the changes will be when it withdraws or injects reserves. However, over a period of several quarters or a year, the "relationship is fairly predictable," says Boehne.

Not only are reserve requirements at nonmember banks a hodgepodge that varies from state to state; the Fed has a hard time getting timely, accurate data on deposits at nonmember banks. Member banks report deposits on a daily basis, but nonmembers report their deposits only four times a year (to the Federal Deposit Insurance Corporation, whose members include all but about 200 of the 13,964 commercial banks). Between reporting dates, the money-supply managers must guess the level of nonmember-bank deposits. As a result, there's a double lag: one between the time of the Fed's action and its effect on the overall money supply and a second before the Fed finds out what that impact was.

To illustrate how far off the Fed can be, Boehne notes that the estimate for the growth in the money supply in 1972 was 8.3 per cent and in 1973, 5 per cent. When nonmember data became available, these figures were revised to 8.7 per cent for 1972 and 5.7 per cent for 1973. For shorter periods the differences are greater. For the second half of 1972 the growth rate of the money supply was revised from 8.5 per cent to 9.4 per cent, and for the first half of 1973, from 6 per cent to 7.7 per cent.

"At a time when the economy was rapidly nearing its capacity to produce, a monetary policy was significantly more expansive than had been thought to be the case when policy was being made," said Boehne.

He called on Congress to solve the data problem simply by allowing the Fed to put nonmember banks on the same daily-reporting basis as member banks.

Another bothersome variable in conducting monetary policy is the float. When checks are processed through the Federal Reserve System, deposits are credited immediately or at most within a day or two of receipt. However, it usually takes longer before the banks that issued the checks are charged for the items. This means that new reserves are created for some banks without the offsetting reduction of reserves of other banks. This float can be anywhere from $2 billion to $4 billion and is sometimes a fairly volatile item.

In January of 1974, the float was $3,385,000,000 out of total bank reserves of $36,655,000,000. By the end of May, the float was down to $2,104,000,000 out of total reserves of $40,133,000,000.

A good part of the volatility of the float can be traced to seasonal patterns of money movements. Payment activity varies with the Christmas shopping season, due dates for tax payments and the like.

"The magnitude of the float isn't too important," a Fed officer explained; "we can adjust to that. It's the sudden changes that bother us. A heavy snowstorm or an airport in Chicago shut down by fog can make a shambles of estimates of the monetary aggregates."

Another aspect of the dual banking system complicates the Federal Reserve's money-management job. As Boehne noted in his article, some state banks can use U.S. securities as part of their reserves. If these state banks are buying Government securities at the same time the Fed is selling them in an effort to contract reserves, open-market operations are being frustrated—at least to the extent of the state-bank purchases.

In day-to-day operations, the Fed feeds out money and soaks it up the way an angler might play a sailfish. When the line gets taut he lets out a little, and when there's slack he reels in.

But too often the Fed must pull in when the line is tight, creating the type of money crunch that was so painful in 1966, 1969–70 and 1974. When the economy is running flat out, it has an insatiable appetite for money. If the Fed keeps feeding it, inflation is aggravated. If it doesn't, interest rates soar, savings banks lose deposits, mortgage money disappears and the economy moves toward recession.

The Fed must know how far it can go before the whole economy blows, so between the technical problems of controlling the money supply and the theoretical ones, the money managers really earn that $5 billion a year.

The U.S. Treasury is also a headache for the monetary authorities. When the Treasury needs money, it's up to the Federal Reserve System to see that the money is there. The Fed is forbidden by law to make direct purchases of new issues of Federal obligations, so it can't directly underwrite Treasury issues. But it doesn't have to. If there is any problem marketing a new Government issue, the Fed buys up old ones, thus opening up the market for the new. It is also very active in the market for Treasury Bills—Treasury obligations which mature within one year and which are sold every week. The Fed bids weekly to roll over its portfolio— that is, replace all maturing issues with new ones.

(Treasury bills are sold at a discount, with the interest paid by pricing the bill below face value. Treasury certificates also have maturities of up to one year, but interest is paid by coupon attached to the security. Longer-term Federal obligations are notes which range in maturity between one year and seven years, and bonds, which go out beyond seven years.)

Technically, the Fed people tell me, they can finance Government deficits without increasing the money supply, but realistically, they can't. Any effort to keep the Treasury money out of the money stock will cause interest rates to fly. As Federal deficits have become a way of life, the Fed is faced with a nearly impossible task: it must keep interest rates reasonable and still finance the demands of the Treasury and the needs of the private sector. In 1974, as in earlier money crunches, something had to give. It came in the form of a squeeze on private business and record-high interest rates. The high rates applied to the Treasury as well as everyone else, but the Government got its money, albeit, as one Fed official said, "grudgingly."

The Fed has not yet perfected a technique for printing red money, as suggested by Francine I. Neff when she became Treasurer of the United States in the summer of 1974. Watching the first batch of green bills bearing her name roll off the presses, Ms. Neff commented that it might be a good idea to print red money to remind the public of budget deficits. She said she thought the bills would look better printed in red and would be a "reminder to put responsibility where it belongs"—on the citizens who constantly demand more government services.

With all the effort expended to control the money supply, there is still disagreement as to just how effective juggling money is in controlling our economic destiny. The argument is as old as chickens and eggs.

Will an increase in the money supply create increased economic activity, or does an increase in activity lead to a bigger money supply?

Also, does price inflation result from a too-rapid increase in the money supply, or do increasing prices pull more money into the stream?

The confirmed monetarists believe that the money supply

is the great moving force for economic activity and a too-rapid increase in the money stock is the fundamental cause of inflation. They cite studies that have found that price inflation was always preceded by a sharp increase in the money supply. From this they infer that the larger money supply had caused prices to rise. My own feeling is that these studies are as significant as the discovery that before every flood since the days of Noah's Ark, there was a striking rise in the water level.

There's another flaw in those quantitative monetary theories. Purchasing power—or, as the economists say, "effective demand"—is equal to the amount of money available and the velocity at which it circulates. The same dollar spent three times during a day will have the same impact on prices as $3 spent once during the same period.

Money doesn't stand still any more than anything else in the economy, and getting a handle on velocity is a slippery business.

Despite the aforementioned reservations about monetary theory, it is fairly obvious that the supply of money has an important impact on the economy, but that impact is not nearly as precise as the monetarists would have you believe.

And during a period of double-digit inflation, there is an extra dimension to be considered in deciding on a proper long-range money-growth target. When prices are increasing at a 10 per cent rate and the money stock is being increased at 8 per cent (a relatively high rate by monetarist standards), is this an expansive policy or a restrictive one? It could be argued (and has been argued) that the "real" money supply is shrinking because it's not keeping up with inflation.

In February of 1973 when the economy was inflating, but at a much slower rate than in the post–oil-price-rise era, Milton Friedman, writing in the Morgan Guaranty Survey, was recommending that the money supply be increased at an annual rate somewhere between 5 and 7 per cent. This, he said, would provide 3 or 4 per cent for growth in real output and 2 or 3 per cent to adjust for inflation.

Following the Friedman formula in the first half of 1974, when inflation was racing along at better than 10 per cent, the money stock should have been growing at 13 to 14 per cent to provide for 3 to 4 per cent real growth and also adjust for inflation. The actual rate reported by the Fed in July for the first half of the year was 7.6 per cent. I don't know about Milton Friedman, but I know that Federal Reserve Board Chairman Arthur Burns would have exploded if the growth rate had been anywhere near the 13 to 14 per cent level. Even the seat of my pants, the source of all this economic wisdom, would have been more than a trifle scorched if money were being pumped out that fast.

There's also a nagging fear that in a real depression increasing the money supply may not revive the economy. It could be like pushing on a string. During the Great Depression of the 1930's there were piles of excess reserves in the banking system, but business was dormant and there was no incentive to get the money into productive use. It just lay idle with the rest of the economy.

IV

THE INTERNATIONAL MONETARY SYSTEM

CHAOS WITH A COLLEGE EDUCATION

The system under which merchandise and money move across national borders appears so complex that most of us make no effort to understand it. All this talk about revaluations, devaluations, Special Drawing Rights, international liquidity, gold convertibility, two-tier systems, parity adjustments, snakes in tunnels, currency floats, dollar overhangs— it's enough to blow the mind. Besides, what difference does it make in my life?

For openers, the system does have a profound effect on your life because it affects the price you pay for everything from Volkswagens to panty hose; and furthermore, it's not all that complex. It's been my belief that international bankers and economists have a vested interest in keeping the general public in the dark about their marvelous machinations. This chapter will lift the veil of secrecy and expose the international conspiracy of obfuscation.

The monetary system set up during World War II at Bretton Woods, New Hampshire, was fractured fatally on August 15, 1971, the day President Nixon said he was "temporarily" suspending the convertibility of the dollar into gold. Up until that point, the dollar was measured in terms of gold, and all the other currencies in the non-Communist world were measured in terms of the dollar. In effect, the dollar was the yardstick used to measure the value of other currencies, and if a foreigner wanted to cash in his dollars for gold, he could do so at $35 an ounce.

This made the dollar a unique currency. While other currencies could be revalued or devalued on the basis of their international financial standing, the dollar just had to sit still because it was locked into gold. In the early days of the Bretton Woods plan, the dollar was so strong that it could remain calm while all others about it were losing their heads. The American economy was powerful while Europe and Japan were being rebuilt out of the wreckage of the war. We had more than half the entire world's supply of monetary gold, and we were selling foreigners so much more than we were buying from them that we could give away billions and still have a favorable payments balance. But this changed in the 60's, and so began the breakdown of the monetary system, set up with such high hopes as World War II was drawing to an end.

While the Bretton Woods agreement was built around the U.S. dollar, it was the devaluation of the British pound in November of 1967 that started the system coming unstuck.

The British devaluation was preceded and followed by frantic gold speculation. This became so intense that the speculators cracked the London gold pool, and in March of 1968 the two-tier gold market was established.

When the free-market gold price split from the official price, it was evident that something was out of whack. Here the U.S. Government was saying that the dollar was worth $\frac{1}{35}$ of an ounce of gold and the free market was saying no. As the price of free-market gold moved up, it was telling the world that the dollar was worth only $\frac{1}{40}$ of an ounce of gold or $\frac{1}{45}$ of an ounce or only $\frac{1}{180}$ of an ounce. This was no way to run an international monetary system.

The traditional requirements of a successful reserve currency (a currency universally acceptable in payment of international debts) were a productive economy, a wealth of resources, a strong military capability to defend those resources and convertibility into a precious metal—gold. Until the two-tier gold market was set up, we had it all. But once there were two gold prices, the quality of convertibility was diluted, and as time went on the dilution increased.

As I pointed out in a prior chapter, convertibility into gold isn't really important in a rational system, but three billion people were unaware of this, and the dollar fell into disrepute as the cornerstone of the system.

How did we get into this mess? Primarily through inertia, self-indulgence and a rather expensive war in Southeast Asia. As a nation, we acted in much the same manner as we did as individuals: we bought too much and overextended ourselves.

If we overspend as individuals, there will be a department-store credit manager or a bank loan officer who'll say, "Hey, wait a minute. You'd better pay up what you owe now or at least get your balance down to a reasonable level before you go borrowing more." Internationally, the function of the credit manager is performed more subtly. There was a run out of the dollar into gold or into currencies our creditors had more faith in.

An individual who can't possibly pay off his debts goes into bankruptcy. A country devalues.

The primary purpose of a devaluation is to make the goods and services of the devaluating country cheaper in terms of the products of other countries and thus increase exports, keep domestic industry humming and improve the balance of payments. It also has some side effects. One is that foreigners holding the devalued currency take a financial beating, since it will buy less anywhere except in the country doing the devaluing.

Also, for the short term, a devaluation aggravates the imbalance it was designed to correct. The immediate effect of devaluation is to increase the cost of imports, but there is a lag before the higher costs discourage purchases abroad. Exports become cheaper immediately, but it takes time before the price change attracts enough buyers to increase volume. With higher-priced imports and lower-priced exports, the balance-of-payments deficit gets worse instead of better.

The United States has not had much experience with devaluations because of the strength of its economy and the fact that foreign trade represents a relatively small proportion of the U.S. economy. Only about 10 per cent of our Gross National Product is represented by imports and exports, while for countries like Germany or Japan the figure would be more than 50 per cent.

Furthermore, under Bretton Woods there was no way for the United States to devalue without undermining the whole system—and when we were forced to devalue, we did break the system. While other countries could change the values of their currencies in terms of the dollar—as the British did in 1967, changing the pound from $2.70 to $2.40—the dollar could be devalued only by raising the official price of gold. And even this would have had no real impact on the position of the dollar against other currencies unless our trading partners were willing to make upward adjustments of their currencies. In other words, the dollar could not be devalued unless other countries agreed to revalue. Otherwise, raising the price of gold would accomplish nothing of substance.

It was for this reason that on August 15, 1971, when President Nixon broke the dollar's link to gold and set our currency afloat, he also imposed a 10 per cent surcharge on American imports. This surcharge was a bargaining weapon to ensure that our trading partners would accept a dollar devaluation. A 10 per cent import tax has the same competitive effect in the domestic market as a 10 per cent devaluation, since it raises the price of foreign goods sold here by 10 per cent.

Domestic products then have an advantage over foreign. Imports will decline while exports continue, and the balance-of-payments position is improved. However, the danger always exists that other nations will retaliate with import taxes of their own, eliminating the advantage and drying up trade in the process.

In the case of the United States, the tax was removed under the Smithsonian agreement, reached in December of 1971, which effectively devalued the dollar and which President Nixon called the greatest financial agreement in monetary history. Dollar devaluation was accomplished through the revaluation upward of the currencies of major industrial countries by an average of 11 to 12 per cent against the dollar. The United States agreed to revalue gold from $35 an ounce to $38—a meaningless gesture. In changing the gold price, the United States was saying that instead of the dollar's not being convertible into gold at $35 an ounce, it is now not convertible at $38 an ounce. Fourteen months later, the United States made it possible not to convert dollars into gold at $42.22 an ounce.

How much a country spends and how much it earns or has the potential to earn will ultimately determine what happens to its currency internationally. Vigorous growth in postwar Germany and Japan and their ability to produce for export markets at prices below those of competing nations resulted in huge balance-of-payments surpluses and strong currency. Britain's aging industry and chronic payments deficits kept the pound under constant downward pressure.

While Germany and Japan were busily honing their economies and tying up foreign markets, the United States was enjoying the position of the number one economic and military power, buying up foreign industry, spreading the gospel of the Harvard Business School, handing out foreign aid, maintaining a military presence around the world (defense expenditures by Germany and Japan ranged from negligible to nonexistent) and spending billions on tourism.

Immediately after World War II, we were the only major industrial power with an economy that was still intact, and we took on the job of rebuilding the rest of the world. The dollars were poured into Europe and Japan and were more than welcome because they represented a claim on an economy whose productive capacity was creating goods they all vitally needed. Thus the dollar was much sought after, and there was little concern over the build-up of dollar balances overseas. Dollars were better than gold, and at any point during the late 40's, the entire decade of the 50's and most of the 60's, any country that wanted to exchange dollars for gold could do so with no trouble. The United States stood ready to move its gold from one bin to another down in the basement of the Federal Reserve Bank of New York under the eyes and machine guns of the Fed's security forces. Over the years there was much bin shifting, until the United States called a halt when its hoard dwindled from $25 billion to $10.5 billion.

U.S. deficits were piling on top of deficits, Europe and Japan grew stronger and stronger and it appeared that there was no way to reverse the process. Instead of the United States' dollar helping finance the rest of the world, we were being accused of exporting inflation, and the French were screaming about being forced to finance the United States' deficit. As William McChesney Martin said in 1968, the United States' deficit was like the man who came to dinner. "Though invited, it stayed too long."

All this activity during the postwar years produced the "dollar overhang." By 1973 there were about $70 billion in the hands of foreign governments and central banks and somewhere between $20 billion and $30 billion in private hands. These dollars were no longer convertible into gold, and the question of what to do about this money preoccupied the thinking of monetary experts from about 1968 until the oil crisis struck, and the figures bounced about in anticipation of Arab riches relegated the dollar overhang to the international petty-cash drawer. There is a vague plan for the conversion of overhang dollars into SDR's at some point in the future, but the excitement has gone out of the issue.

There is an irreconcilable conflict on the question of deficits and surpluses. It seems every country wants to run a surplus in its balance of payments, but there's this mathematical principle that keeps getting in the way. No matter how hard the world tries, not even the cleverest of experts has been able to devise a system under which everybody can have a surplus. Somehow one country's surplus invariably shows up as a deficit somewhere else. About the best that can be devised is a system that self-adjusts so that surplus countries will raise their prices and slow down their economies while deficit countries will lower prices and speed up their economies. And here is the gut of the problem in coming up with a workable system. What about a country that's running a deficit in international payments but needs to slow down its domestic economy to keep inflation from running away with itself?

But more about that later. Realistically, a deficit in a nation's balance of payments isn't all that bad, so long as the rest of the world is willing to put up with it. A deficit country is getting more than it's giving. The United States really had a ball during all those deficit years. We bought up huge chunks of foreign industry. Direct investment of U.S. corporations overseas went from $31.8 billion in 1960 to $78.1 billion in 1970. We were able to provide stereo sets and transistor radios from Japan for every blue-jeaned kid in the country. We traveled all over the world spreading our dollars in hotels and souvenir shops from Paris to Pretoria, and it was quite a jolt for American tourists when during the periodic money crises in the late 60's and early 70's, they found they couldn't cash their dollar-denominated traveler's checks or had to cash them at a smashing discount.

Until the world discovered what was happening, we were enjoying internationally the same kind of buy-now-pay-later life style that was so popular at home.

The unpleasantness of being constantly in debt doesn't hit until the bills start flooding in and there's no money to pay them with. This is followed by more unpleasantness as creditors started hollering for their money.

In the case of the American dollar, signs that foreigners had had enough of providing us with real assets in exchange for our paper dollars showed up in the flight of capital out of the dollar into gold or into strong currencies, particularly the West German mark.

On a number of occasions, Germany had to buy up billions in dollars in an effort to support the price of the dollar at the levels agreed upon under Bretton Woods. In the end, speculators who were buying marks for dollars in the hope of profiting from upward revaluation of the mark forced the revaluation. From a practical standpoint, there were just so many marks the Germans could exchange for dollars without destroying their own economy because these newly created marks found their way into the domestic money supply. Such massive creation of marks would lead to a disastrous inflation if continued for any length of time. The supply of dollars created through the years of deficits which were sloshing around Europe in what came to be the Eurodollar market and the vast resources of the multinational corporations provided a source of speculation that was too strong for the German Central Bank to contain. Here was another crack in the Bretton Woods plan.

Through the postwar years, as the U.S. balance-of-payments deficits were becoming chronic, we still managed to maintain a favorable balance of trade—we were exporting more goods than we imported. Until 1971, that is. It was a real shocker to learn that not only did the United States have a deficit in the over-all balance of payments, but for the first time in this century we were buying more goods from foreigners than we sold overseas.

The over-all deficit in 1971 was $10 billion in our "basic" balance of payments. The "basic" balance is regarded as the most realistic of the several methods of international accounting. It takes in all international transactions except the short-term movements of speculative capital that have a tendency to distort the basic forces in operation. It was adopted by the Department of Commerce in 1960 and has served us well in periods when international speculators were fleeing from the dollar into stronger currencies.

There are three other balance-of-payments measures: current account, net liquidity and official reserve. Since the basic balance is always described as the most "meaningful" measure and since this whole subject can get pretty technical and boring, I hope you'll forgive me for not trying to explain the other three.

Anyhow, that year the United States imported $45.5 billion worth of goods and exported only $42.8 billion, for a trade deficit of $2.7 billion.

The switch of our trade account from the black into the red resulted from a long-term trend of increasing imports at a much faster pace than the rise in exports. In the nine-year period from 1964 through 1972, U.S. imports increased 197 per cent, from $18.7 billion to $55.5 billion, while exports were increasing 90 per cent, from $25.8 billion to $49.1 billion.

Although the trade deficit was the most dramatic development in our foreign accounts in 1971, it was only the beginning of our payments problems that year.

We also paid $1.5 billion to foreigners for services such as shipping and insurance; tourism and foreign travel cost us another $5.5 billion, and some $1.5 billion in Social Security payments and other overseas remittances added to the deficit; there was $2.4 billion in bank loans to foreigners; Americans bought $900 million worth of foreign securities and U.S. corporations invested $4.8 billion in overseas operations; foreigners received interest and dividend payments of $4.9 billion on their U.S. investments; we paid out $6.2 billion in foreign aid and loans (in the early postwar years, this item was more than covered by our favorable trade balance) and we spent $4.8 billion overseas on military operations.

On the income side of the ledger, foreigners paid Americans $1.8 billion for our services (a net plus of $300 million); foreign travelers here paid out $3.1 billion ($2.4 billion less than we spent overseas); foreigners bought $2.3 billion in U.S. securities (chalk up a $1.4 billion edge for Wall Street over foreign stock markets); foreign direct investment in the U.S. came to $100 million, or about $4.7 billion less than we invested abroad; foreign governments repaid $2.1 billion in debts to us, or about $4.1 billion less than we paid out in foreign aid and finally, U.S. corporate investments overseas brought in $9.4 billion—principally the fruits of the great postwar surge of foreign investment by U.S.-based multinational corporations.

After a second devaluation of the dollar by about 10 per cent in February of 1973—this we accomplished by persuading other major nations again to upvalue their currencies and by raising the official price of gold from $38 an ounce to $42.22—the United States finally reported a surplus in its basic balance of payments in 1973, primarily as a result of a $7.6 billion swing in our trade balance. For the year 1973, the U.S. Department of Commerce announced that the basic balance of payments had turned around from a $9.8 billion deficit in 1972 to a $1.2 billion surplus.

This was good news for the dollar, although it later turned out that the whole thing was a mistake. Indeed, there had been a sharp improvement in the payments position of the United States, but the reported surplus was a bit optimistic. In June of 1974, while announcing a record first-quarter $2.1 billion surplus in the basic balance, the Commerce Department added a postscript. Revised figures for 1973 showed that instead of a surplus of $1.2 billion, there had been a deficit of $744 million. The revision involved a sharp cut in the figure that had been reported originally for oil-company earnings overseas and some "adjustments of seasonal factors."

Furthermore, the higher cost of imported petroleum had resulted in a new deterioration of our trade account. While the fourth quarter of 1973 had shown a $1.3 billion trade surplus, the first quarter of 1974 produced a trade figure only $101 million in the black. And what do you think was responsible for most of the record first-quarter balance-of-payments surplus? Higher earnings of the foreign affiliates of the U.S. oil companies, the same item so drastically revised in the 1973 figures.

Whatever happens to the U.S. balance of payments in the years to come, it is clear that the dollar is no longer a currency of such overwhelming strength that it can be used as the principal international reserve asset. The world is no longer willing to have most of its reserves tied up in claims against the United States.

Without any official agreements or proclamations, once the dollar got into trouble stronger currencies were replacing it as an international reserve. In September of 1973, monetary expert C. Fred Bergsten, a senior fellow at the Brookings Institution, pointed out that the West German mark was increasingly being used as a reserve currency. He noted that the mark had surpassed sterling as the second most widely used currency in the world for both private transactions and official reserves (the dollar was still number one) and that German per capita income and total exports had equaled those of the United States. And furthermore, the mark had been appreciating while the dollar had been depreciating.

Bergsten also expressed the opinion that the then-functioning European float, or snake in the tunnel, whereby a group of currencies were kept within a band of 2¼ per cent from each other, was a *de facto* "mark zone" and not an operation of the Common Market.

"French political purposes are served by referring to the operation as 'European' and it is uncertain whether France will remain a participant when it becomes clear that the operation is instead a mark zone," Bergsten said.

Four months after Bergsten made this statement, France dropped out of the "snake" and let the franc float downward to help French exports. Whether the mark's dominance of the snake had anything to do with the French decision was not clear.

The strength of the mark proved almost as much of a problem as the weakness of the dollar in shattering the remnants of Bretton Woods.

Under that old international agreement, it was the responsibility of each country to maintain the value of its own currency within a range of 1 per cent above or below an agreed value. When a currency started to move downward, the nation's central bank went into the exchange markets and bought its own currency to support the price. If the currency was going up in value and threatened to break out of the upper limit, the central bank would go out and sell its currency.

In practice, the support programs of the central banks, known in the trade as intervention, meant buying and selling dollars. If the mark was going up, the Bundesbank went out and bought dollars (sold marks), and if the mark was going down, the German central bank would sell dollars (buy marks). It's all very confusing, but it worked as long as any one currency didn't become so strong or so weak that it broke out of the band. If this happened, there was nothing left to do but have a crisis. Exchange markets closed; bankers flew on emergency meetings, usually to Basel, Switzerland, and when the smoke cleared, there was either a revaluation or a devaluation, and a new central rate or parity fixed, and calm was restored until the next crisis.

The United States stood aloof from all this buying and selling because its currency was the hub of the system and you just don't go moving the hub around. It was not until July, 1973, after two formal devaluations of the dollar and nearly two years after the Bretton Woods arrangement was effectively scrapped by the ending of convertibility, that the United States began to take an active role intervening in exchange markets in support of the dollar.

The second devaluation of the dollar on February 12, 1973, failed to calm the exchange markets for more than a few days. By February 23, the dollar had hit bottom against major European currencies in terms of the new lower levels set under the devaluation agreement. By this time, the dollar could fluctuate in a range of 2¼ per cent above or below its parity, but even this wasn't enough. On Thursday, March 1, more than $3.6 billion was dumped on European central banks—mostly German—and the exchanges were closed to regroup. They reopened on March 19 after the mark had been revalued upward by 3 per cent and a plan adopted for a joint float of the currencies of five members of the European Community—Germany, France, Belgium, the Netherlands and Denmark. Norway and Sweden later joined. These nations agreed to float their currencies in a bloc against the dollar and keep the relationships with each other within a band of 2¼ per cent.

This was the snake in the tunnel that hip international money types talked about. The snake represented the European currencies that could wiggle within the 2¼ per cent band in the tunnel which represented the wider band—4½ per cent—that the rest of the world's currencies could move up and down in.

Despite the arrangements made in March, instability continued, and by May another speculative run broke out. The German mark kept moving up and pulling the other European currencies in the snake up with it. On June 29 the mark was revalued again, this time by 5½ per cent. By July 6 the mark was 30 per cent higher than the level set after the February devaluation of the dollar, and other European currencies were up between 18 and 21 per cent. And during all this monetary turmoil, gold had shot up to $127 on the London bullion market.

During July the exchange markets were in an almost continuous state of crisis and some New York banks were refusing to quote rates on certain European currencies. Trading in foreign exchange was coming to a halt.

At that point, the Federal Reserve Bank of New York, which handles the foreign-exchange functions for the U.S. Treasury and the Federal Reserve System, negotiated an increase in its line of international credit to $18 billion and it moved directly into the exchange markets to shore up the dollar. The credit line was negotiated through the so-called "swap network" made up of the central banks of the major financial powers.

The network is an arrangement in which the central banks swap currencies for short periods for use in stabilizing exchange fluctuations. By April of 1974, the credit line available through the network was increased to $20 billion. U.S. borrowings from the network outstanding as of April 30, 1974, were $1.6 billion, so there was lots of room to go higher.

The size of the pool of funds available to defend the dollar, plus active participation of the New York Fed in the exchange markets, quieted things down for a while. There was also some help from an unexpected (and unwelcome) source —the Arab oil embargo in October, 1973.

The oil crisis had the effect of strengthening the dollar because the United States was considered less vulnerable than the other two financial superpowers, Germany and Japan. While the United States was a large importer of oil, it was also the world's largest petroleum producer. (In May, 1974, the United States fell to number two as Saudi Arabia produced 8.7 million barrels a day to our 8.5 million.) Germany and Japan were almost entirely dependent on imported oil. By January of 1974 the dollar had floated upward to the point of virtually wiping out the effects of the February devaluation against some currencies.

But the dollar's strength didn't last long. Market sentiment shifted, and at the end of January the dollar began another sharp decline. The Federal Reserve Bank attributed the reversal to the removal of controls on the export of U.S. capital (the controls were put in by the Johnson Administration in 1968 to help fight balance-of-payments deficits); a drop in interest rates here while rates abroad remained high, having the effect of attracting money overseas; and a new look at the impact of the energy crisis.

Said the New York Fed in its June report on foreign-exchange operations for the first four months of 1974: ". . . the energy crisis threatened to provoke a more rapid and pronounced deterioration in our trade balances than originally expected, while Germany showed a continuing surplus of surprising strength."

As a result, the dollar dropped about 17 per cent against the mark from the January peak through the end of April.

Direct intervention by the Federal Reserve in support of the dollar was an admission that the United States had abandoned all pretense of retaining the dollar's position as a super currency. The United States was conceding that the dollar's link to $42.22 gold was the fiction everyone knew it was. The dollar was another currency floating in the market place, and the float was being managed by the Federal Reserve in the same manner in which the floating mark was managed by the Bundesbank or the pound was being supported by the Bank of England.

Even the appearance of stability of value required for a reserve currency was no longer applicable to the dollar.

Now the world was looking for a replacement, and most of the attention was focused on SDR's—Special Drawing Rights, that mysterious international money that was originally promoted as "paper gold."

The SDR's were originally designed as a means of supplying international liquidity. This is a fancy way of saying that SDR's would be used to expand the international money supply as needed to support the expansion of international business. By the time the first SDR's were issued, the international wits were saying that with the huge supply of dollars arising from our string of deficits, the world already was "drowning in liquidity."

It was hoped that SDR's would overcome the basic flaws in a system dependent on a reserve currency or on gold. The trouble with gold—besides the facts that it's cumbersome, it's useless and its value is founded more on superstition than reality—is that its supply is limited and there's no way to increase the supply in tandem with the increase in world trade. A reserve currency, on the other hand, can be expanded as it is needed to support growing trade. But as the supply of a reserve currency expands, it begins to destroy itself.

If a nation is to supply its currency as reserves for the rest of the world, it does so by running balance-of-payments deficits. The dollar reserves used by other countries were the mirror image of the deficits the United States piled up in the postwar years. Yet as these deficits mounted, faith in the dollar deteriorated. Catch-22.

Special Drawing Rights were created for the first time in

1969 by the International Monetary Fund, a group of 126 member nations that had its origins in the Bretton Woods agreement. SDR's were allocated to various members based on their shares in the IMF.

There was great difficulty in explaining what SDR's were. Were SDR's equivalent to gold? Was an SDR cash or a form of credit? Was an SDR just a bookkeeping entry in the IMF ledgers?

In the beginning they were referred to as "paper gold" for two reasons: because their value was denominated in terms of gold and for public relations purposes. To have a little of the gold mystique rub off on SDR's wouldn't hurt. The question of whether SDR's were money or credit was conveniently ducked by comparing the SDR to a zebra: it can just as accurately be described as a black animal with white stripes or a white animal with black stripes, said Otmar Emminger, a West German monetary expert and enthusiastic supporter of the SDR's.

Pierre-Paul Schweitzer, managing director of the IMF at the time the SDR's were introduced, agreed with Emminger but added that what you call them is not important. The important thing is how SDR's can be used.

"Their value," said Schweitzer,

will derive essentially from the fact that participants will be obliged to accept them when properly transferred and to provide in exchange convertible currency or gold, up to a point where they are holding three times as many Special Drawing Rights as have been allocated them by the Fund. The acceptance limit was set at this level in order to ensure that, on any reasonable view, the scheme would be endowed with a sufficient margin of liquidity.

The value of SDR's was fixed in 1969 at .888671 of a gram of fine gold, the gold equivalent of the dollar. On December 18, 1971, with the Smithsonian agreement, the dollar was devalued 7.89 per cent in terms of gold, thus being cut down to .818513 of a gram of gold. The February, 1973, devaluation further reduced the dollar equivalent in gold to .736662 of a gram. Through all this, the SDR remained at .888671 of a gram of gold, and thus, in terms of the dollar, the SDR was worth $1.206348. The point of this exercise in six-decimal-place digits is to show that while the dollar was depreciating, the SDR was standing firm, thus demonstrating at least one advantage of this type of international reserve. I should point out that the figures are from a *New York Times* column by John H. Allen, one of the few people I know who seems at home in six decimal places.

In any event, the nations who held dollars in their reserves lost money when the dollar was devalued. The portion of reserves represented by SDR's did not depreciate in terms of gold.

However, the SDR's did depreciate in terms of marks and yen, because these currencies increased in value to a much greater extent than the two official U.S. devaluations reflected. So in the spring of 1974, it was decided to tie the value of SDR's to a "basket" of sixteen major currencies to neutralize the exchange risk between currencies. Although fading fast, the dollar was still the world's leading international currency, and it was given the largest role in the basket —33 per cent. The mark was next with 12.5 per cent. The agreement also provided that the SDR's would draw interest at 5 per cent and the interest rate could be adjusted up or down depending on short-term market rates.

Linking SDR's to a group of currencies instead of gold was another step in the movement to phase gold out of the monetary system. At the same time, there was an agreement to permit official gold reserves to be used as collateral for loans at whatever value the lender was willing to accept. Italy was then running a deficit of around $1 billion a month and was speeding toward bankruptcy. The Italians had a gold hoard of $3.5 billion at the official $42.22 price, but was not about to pay any of it out when the free-market price was almost four times that. Freeing the gold reserves for use as collateral at the market price gave Italy about $12 billion worth of gold to work with instead of $3.5 billion.

In addition to helping bail out Italy, the move further downgraded the standing of the "official" price to that of a complete anachronism.

The value of the SDR's was to be $1.2056 starting on June 28, 1974. The SDR equivalent in other countries would be based on their exchange rates on that day. From that point on, there would be a daily recalculation of the SDR's value in terms of all sixteen currencies through a complex weighted mathematical formula.

As of this writing, there was about $11.5 billion in SDR's outstanding—the appreciated value of the $9.5 billion issued.

It has been suggested by some experts that the IMF be given the power to issue SDR's in unlimited amounts in order to overwhelm a run against any one currency. The IMF would then be in a position to take emergency action to shore up the currency of a bankrupt or nearly bankrupt nation and prevent the kind of chain reaction that the U.S. Fed was able to head off after the Penn Central bankruptcy and the Franklin National Bank failure.

It seems doubtful that the world is ready to grant the IMF the full status of an international central bank. And the IMF's lack of power is what makes the SDR's less than a perfect vehicle for international transactions.

The limited authority of the IMF also figures in the question of whether SDR's represent money or credit—the old zebra bit. Stripped down, the SDR is just a bookkeeping entry. But so is money. The difference between money and credit is based on who is keeping the books. If the U.S. Government through the Federal Reserve System issues a $1 bill, that's a bookkeeping entry and it's also money. If I issue a $1 IOU, it's a bookkeeping entry and it's credit.

If the IMF gets the support of member states and can enforce its bookkeeping entries internationally as our government can domestically, SDR's will become international money. If the IMF doesn't get the international support it needs, the SDR's will be a form of credit and not a very good one.

The original agreement on SDR's provided for a fresh ration of the new reserves to be issued every year. This was done until 1972, when the IMF quietly postponed the issuance until 1973. The major Western nations could not agree on an amount to be created, the monetary system was going through a traumatic change and there was really no need to create any additional international reserves, since in the first nine months of the year nearly $15 billion poured into the world's official reserves reflecting U.S. deficits.

When 1973 came in, the monetary system was still unstable, little progress had been made toward reform and in the fall of that year the oil crisis added a new dimension to the world's monetary problems: what to do about the huge payments surpluses expected by oil-exporting nations and the deficits of the oil-importing nations.

The Arab oil embargo, followed by a fourfold increase in the price of oil, created instant panic in international monetary circles. It was feared that the oil-exporting countries would drain the rest of the world dry in short order. With Arab oil earnings estimated to rise by $65 billion in 1974 alone, every nation in the world, except the large oil exporters, would be running massive payments deficits, and there would be no way ever to restore the world to any state of financial order.

Writing in *The New York Times* in June of 1974, C. Fred Bergsten took a calmer view:

". . . a sizable share of the increased earnings of the oil-exporting countries will be spent on imports from the industrial world," the monetary expert wrote.

Some oil countries will spend virtually all of their increased earnings themselves; all are rapidly revising their development strategies and military plans to do so. Some will lend their money to others who will quickly spend it.

So even the trade balances of the industrial world will not decline by more than, say, half of the increase in its oil bill this year. Those trade balances will be even better in subsequent years, and any further increases in oil countries' earnings are more than offset by their increased imports. Indeed, the United States appears to have already reached its new plateau of oil imports in April at an annual rate of $27 billion, but there was a surplus in over-all trade as exports reached an annual rate of almost $100 billion.

. . . the prophets of doom confuse the balance of trade and the balance of payments. They ignore the simple but central fact that the oil exporters must invest in the industrial world any of their increased earnings that they do not spend. The Arabs will not bury the money in the ground. Thus, there can be no deficit in the balance of payments of the industrial world as a whole.

David Rockefeller, the internationally minded chairman of Chase Manhattan Bank, was not so sanguine about the balance-of-payments picture. Rockefeller projected a $60 billion surplus for oil-producing nations in 1974 (compared with $4 billion in 1973), building their reserves to over $70 billion by year end, to $140 billion by the end of 1975 and to $200 billion by the end of 1976. He said he couldn't see how these reserves could be smoothly recycled without some new international machinery.

Looking farther into the future than Rockefeller, Minos A. Zombanakis, managing director of First Boston (Europe), Ltd., the investment-banking firm, estimated that by 1984, Saudi Arabia, Kuwait, Abu Dhabi, Libya and Iraq would have accumulated a staggering $500 billion in "surplus revenues."

To put the figure in perspective, Zombanakis pointed out that at the time (June, 1974) the world's total official reserves came to about $165 billion.

What were the Arabs going to do with all this money? At

a seminar sponsored by *The Financial Times* of London at
the Waldorf Astoria Hotel in New York, Dr. M. M. Abushadi,
the chairman of Union de Banques Arabes et Françaises, a
French-based consortium which includes twenty-six Arab
banks, explained what the Arabs would like to do with the
money. First, he said, they will spend about 20 per cent of
the $600 billion expected to be amassed over the decade in
their home economies.

Abushadi, once chairman of the National Bank of Egypt,
estimated that $100 billion or so would be as much as these
countries could absorb domestically. This would leave about
$500 billion to be spent elsewhere. (The $600 billion figure
for Arab revenues over the decade seems to have become
the standard estimate, so it's probably wrong.) After expenditures at home, Abushadi said, the Arab oil countries
would invest in Arab countries that have no oil. These countries, he said, "have a large capacity for absorbing investments on a profitable basis." Next, he said, the oil countries
will seek investments in Africa and other "third world" areas
"on the basis of common interests and attracted by the lucrative investments in a number of these countries."

The Arabs will also be looking for "safe hedge investments" such as gold, diamonds and real estate and expect to
place large sums in bank deposits and government securities. What they will be particularly anxious to obtain on such
investments are "guarantees against inflation and currency
devaluation."

Abushadi warned:

> The absence of such guarantees could have severe repercussions on
> international monetary stability since investors would be bound to shift
> from one currency to the other, causing disturbances in capital markets.
> I believe this question warrants particular attention in any future
> international monetary reform.

The Arab banker was making it clear that the monetary
system then in place was a fragile mechanism that the Arabs

could bust any time they chose. But he added that the Arabs were aware that "income maximization could only be achieved through their keen interest in the stability of the international monetary system depending partly on their investment behavior and largely on the growth of the world economy."

American banker Rockefeller spread his fears on the record at an international monetary conference sponsored by the American Bankers Association at Williamsburg, Virginia, in June of 1974, just a few days before Mr. Abushadi's talk.

Rockefeller noted that while some oil countries such as Iran, Venezuela, Nigeria and Indonesia have the long-run capacity to spend their oil revenue for national development, countries such as Saudi Arabia and Kuwait, which will be earning the bulk of the oil money, do not. One of the major aims of the Arab countries, said Rockefeller, "is eventually to accumulate a body of invested wealth outside their countries which will yield an income great enough to replace their oil reserve as it runs out."

Rockefeller conceded some validity to the argument that the forces of supply and demand will bring oil prices down while inflation will help bring other products and services up, so that a new equilibrium will be established. However, he said that the purchases of the large oil producers are relatively small, so inflation won't be enough to close the gap, and relying on supply and demand to bring the price of oil down could "have disastrous results" for the economies of the developed nations. "Moreover, if the position of the developed nations is eroded further, the developing nations can have little hope at all," he said.

There is no way of telling, at this point, whether Bergsten's confidence or Rockefeller's alarm is the more appropriate stance. I lean toward confidence, since it seems to me that nothing fundamental has happened to make oil worth four times what it was selling for in 1973.

If a gallon of gas is worth a loaf of bread and suddenly the seller of gas decides that his product is worth four loaves of bread, it won't be too long before the seller of bread catches up—either by an increase in the bread price or by a decline in the gas price. While on a global scale this relationship is obscured by a lot of technical jargon, it exists and should ultimately prevail. Furthermore, nothing comes easier to an individual or a nation than learning to spend new-found riches.

Meanwhile, the search goes on for a new monetary system, one that can deal with the twin problems of the fall of the dollar and the sudden riches of the oil exporters. There are some experts who think that the best way to reform the system is to let it alone, with every currency floating against every other and the devil take the hindmost. But the consensus appears to be in favor of either a carefully managed floating system or a renewal of the fixed-rates system along the lines of Bretton Woods.

The search is for a "stable but flexible" system—an obvious contradiction that doesn't bother the experts.

A system of floating currencies implies that the relative value of each currency will float up and down in response to supply and demand. Theoretically, a "clean float" is self-adjusting. When a currency gets strong, its price goes up. This will mean that the strong-currency country will have its products marked up in the competitive world markets and it will begin to lose sales. This will give the weak-currency countries a chance to catch up, and there will be a constant pressure heading each currency toward its equilibrium point.

But since the world is composed of sovereign nations each looking out for its own interests, clean floating remains a theoretical concept that doesn't exist in real life. A nation will let its currency float cleanly only so long as the float serves its national interest. If a country's domestic economy is threatened because the currency is floating in the wrong direction—for instance, the value of the currency is rising during a period of unemployment—the float will soon be manipulated.

This is known as "dirty floating," and that's what any free-floating system is bound to degenerate into.

Between clean floating and dirty floating there is the concept of "managed floating." This involves intervention by central banks to smooth out short-run fluctuations or to moderate speculative swings. A cleanly managed float should not attempt to run counter to fundamental weaknesses or strengths in a currency, but it is often difficult for the naked eye to distinguish managed floating from dirty floating, since one man's fundamental can be another's aberration.

The primacy of national interests over balance-of-payments questions was plainly illustrated by the French in January of 1974. Since the breakdown of Bretton Woods, the French have been most vociferous in pressing for a new system of fixed parities (preferably built around gold at $200 an ounce). Yet when it appeared that if the franc continued to be supported at agreed-upon levels France's domestic growth would be impaired, France showed no hesitation in extricating the franc from the snake in the tunnel and letting it float downward.

Alluding to the French action, Professor Gottfried Haberler, a noted monetary authority, commented that no country "is willing to submit to the balance-of-payments discipline which it preaches to others." Nevertheless, Professor Haberler advocates managed floating under IMF supervision to keep it clean.

Professor Haberler, Resident Scholar at the American Enterprise Institute and the Galen L. Stone Professor Emeritus of International Trade at Harvard University, thinks there are conditions in the current international economy working against the competitive devaluation pattern of the 1930's.

Using a dirty float to force the value of a nation's currency down, said Professor Haberler, would be inflationary, and the last thing the world needs is more inflation. Furthermore, if a country wants to avoid unemployment and keep its domestic economy growing, it can do so by inflating internally. Finally, if one country starts dumping currency to push the prices down, either we can accept it as a contribution to our own anti-inflation efforts or we can always start dumping our own currency.

Brazil, whose indexed economy is so often used as an example of painless inflation fighting, is also singled out by Professor Haberler as a model in espousing a system of floating exchange rates.

In an article printed by the American Enterprise Institute in June, 1973, Professor Haberler says:

. . . Brazil has had a lot of inflation—20 per cent a year for the last five years. (Now it is down to 15 per cent.) Brazil has therefore had to depreciate the cruzeiro from time to time, or else she would have lost her exports fast. Until 1968 she had an adjustable peg. Every six or seven months the cruzeiro was devalued with a big bang. During the intervals pressure built up, speculation was rife and black markets flourished. In 1968 she adopted not a floating rate but a close substitute to floating, what has become known as a "trotting peg." Under this system the currency is devalued by 1½ or 2 per cent every five or six weeks. This has worked very well. There has been very little speculation because it does not pay to speculate on a parity change of 1–2%, if the precise date and magnitude is not known, when interest rates are over 30% (as they have to be under a highly inflationary situation).

The moral is not that inflation does not matter—the country would be better off without inflation—but that the potentially disastrous consequences of inflation on foreign trade can be avoided or at least greatly mitigated by flexible exchange rates.

The Bretton Woods system was successful through the 1950's and most of the 60's and international trade flourished. With currency values clearly fixed within a range of 1 per cent up or down, goods and capital flowed smoothly through the world. This was in sharp contrast to the 30's, when each country was busily trying to undermine its neighbor through competitive devaluations.

Surprisingly, even after the breakdown and the transition to a system of floating from crisis to crisis, world trade continued to expand.

In 1973, trade increased a startling 36 per cent as total exports hit $510 billion. The figure was not quite as startling when the inflation factor was wrung out, but even after adjustment there was a respectable 12 per cent gain. The International Monetary Fund, which tracks global trade figures and inflation rates, reported that the real increase in trade was "far above the average annual growth in past years" and reflected the general boom in industrial countries during the year.

Businessmen, however, are not comfortable with floating rates. A survey by the Conference Board in early 1973 of 119 business leaders from 42 countries found that most business executives felt "a greater degree of stability in exchange rates is vital if international business is to operate effectively." In explaining the need for stability, the survey quoted a British business leader as stating, "The world monetary system is probably the greatest single factor affecting international trade and investment, and to enable this circulation system to function efficiently, exchange rates must be both realistic and reasonably stable."

At a press briefing in the late spring of 1974, Charles A. Coombs, special manager of the foreign-currency operations of the Federal Reserve System and senior vice-president of the Federal Reserve Bank of New York, said that while the academic community seems delighted with the floating rate system, those dealing with the system on a day-to-day basis feel that they are just "making the best of a difficult situation." He said they were concerned with overtrading and rate manipulation.

Coombs said he felt that world trade continued to increase because of the world-wide boom. With the tremendous demand and the strong seller's market, exchange-rate fluctuations have not been that important. In other words, world trade was growing in spite of unstable currency rates, not because of them.

The arguments against flexible or floating exchange rates are that they add uncertainty to international transactions; they encourage speculation; they tempt governments to use currency fluctuations to avoid making fundamental changes in their domestic economies and they tend to fragment the international community rather than integrate it. Nations should strive for one market, one price and one money, say the fixed-rate enthusiasts.

In taking a jab at Secretary of the Treasury George Shultz upon his retirement from the Nixon Administration in 1974, Democrat John Kenneth Galbraith called the floating-currency arrangement, for which Shultz took some credit, "no design at all." In a letter to *The New York Times,* Galbraith chided, "Dr. Shultz, one fears, would praise himself for inventing chaos."

Those favoring flexible rates say that such an arrangement would absorb temporary pressures and gradually adjust to persistent ones and that market forces add self-correction, not speculation; also, small and frequent changes permit adjustment without the periodic traumas that occurred under the Bretton Woods fixed-parity system whenever a major currency became undervalued or overvalued.

First National City Bank, New York's largest bank and an addict of the monetarist theory of economics, puts much of the blame for the acceleration of inflation in the late 60's and early 70's on the increase in world money supply stemming from the rigidities of the fixed-parity system of Bretton Woods.

"The current wave of worldwide inflation is largely the

result of unsuccessful efforts to maintain a system of fixed exchange rates in the face of powerful market forces that eventually destroyed it," said Citibank in a September, 1973, newsletter.

Fixed parities forced countries to take in billions of dollars to support the price of the dollar in international markets, and these dollars found their way into the money supply, the bank said. In the long run, according to Citibank, a system of floating rates would prevent the export of inflation and make it possible for each country to maintain better control over its own money supply.

Aside from the technicalities, the advantages of stable international currency relationships are apparent. If an American wants to buy some British silverware and has dollars, under a system of fixed exchange rates he knows how many dollars he needs to pay for the merchandise even if there is some delay in completing the transaction.

A system of floating rates adds another variable to a business environment that already has more than its share. Bankers will tell you that floating exchange rates are really no big problem because any businessman can hedge his exchange risks by buying forward or going short or any number of sophisticated financing arrangements. But this costs money, and the only thing a businessman needs less than more variables is higher costs.

Bankers stand to make money under floating rates principally from commissions they earn for handling the hedging operations for clients. But floating rates have also tempted bankers into dangerous speculation. All it takes to make money is a little knowledge of the exchange markets—and who knows these markets better than bankers, who are dealing in currencies all the time?

Regrettably, forecasting the movement of exchange rates is just as difficult as forecasting the stock market or the weather. Franklin National Bank, the twentieth-largest bank in the country with assets of $5 billion, lost something in the neighborhood of $45 million in five months from foreign-exchange trading, much of it unauthorized, and went broke.

A West German private bank with nearly a billion dollars in assets was forced to close in June of 1974 because of foreign-exchange losses. The failure sent out shock waves to foreign-exchange markets everywhere. When a large bank fails to meet its commitments, there's a domino effect that's difficult to contain.

There were some winners in the complex business of buying and selling foreign exchange, too. For instance, the Chase Manhattan Bank, hard pressed to keep up with its rival First National City Bank in earnings growth, did very well in the exchange markets in 1973. For the full year, the bank earned $36.5 million from foreign-exchange trading, more than $16 million over the prior year's trading profits. Currency-trading profits represented 15 per cent of Chase's pretax earnings and about one-third of Chase's overseas profits. For the fourth quarter of the year, exchange-trading profits were even more dramatic; they shot up about 200 per cent over the prior year and represented about 19 per cent of the bank's total pretax profits. In the first quarter of 1974, the trend continued; currency-trading profits more than doubled and came to nearly 25 per cent of pretax income, compared with 11 per cent in the first quarter of 1973.

Chase, of course, denied that it was engaged in "speculation." David Rockefeller told me during an interview that floating rates created an opportunity for profit "and if you know what you're doing, you can make money."

My own feeling is that the difference between speculative profit and trading profits from foreign-exchange dealings is a matter of semantics, and it frightens me to think that the third-largest banking organization in the United States has such a substantial portion of its earnings tied to the vagaries of an international floating crap game.

Just how wrong "knowledgeable" bankers can be about the direction of foreign-exchange rates was illustrated in a couple of predictions by Chemical Bank, one of New York's major banking institutions.

In the January/February, 1974, issue of "Report from Europe," the bank commented on the strength of the dollar since the oil crisis and predicted that the dollar would grow even stronger: "The dominant concern is not *whether* [italics Chemical's] this advance will occur but *when* it will occur. . . ." The bank went on to back up the logic of the prediction: the oil crisis; that shortages and rising prices would affect other countries more than the United States; anticipated U.S. balance-of-payments surpluses and the prospect that the market would shift into dollars in anticipation of these developments.

The prediction turned sour as the dollar plummeted at the end of January. In the very next issue (March/April), Chemical said:

Foreign monetary exchange conditions have been closely tied to the oil situation. Presently, there is a growing awareness among market and financial analysts that neither supply problems nor balance-of-payments impact will be as serious as previously anticipated for most European countries and Japan. As a result, there is a continuing realization that still further weakening of the dollar is possible.

It's a tough market to figure.

The clients for which banks have been so actively trading currencies are to a large extent the multinational corporations. One by-product of the binge of American investment abroad has been the awesome expansion of the multinationals. While multinational corporations are not new or necessarily American-based, the postwar period of the strong dollar gave U.S. corporations an unprecedented opportunity to spread and grow.

It has become fashionable to regard these behemoths as

so powerful that they defy governmental control. ITT is written of as a "sovereign state" and is accused of financing South American revolutions. Just how powerful these corporations are is difficult to assess, but I think there has been some exaggeration. Look at what happened to the international oils when the Arab governments decided to take a larger and larger share of the profits. There was little these corporate giants could do except follow the example of Mobil Oil Corporation, which decided to make an offer to buy Marcor (owner of Montgomery Ward) while there were still some oil profits to be spent.

It has been estimated that the multinationals in 1973 accounted for about 15 per cent of this earth's Gross National Product and that by 1985, about 300 mammoth multinationals would be producing fully half of this world's goods and services—that is, assuming no exogenous variables show up to abort this expected growth.

To head off as many exogenous developments as they can, the multinationals are engaged in a public relations campaign to counter what they feel has been a bad press. They have banded together and financed a number of studies proving that U.S.-based multinational corporations are really a bunch of international Boy Scouts. They create jobs domestically rather than exporting them overseas. They help the U.S. balance of payments by all the money they earn overseas. They don't exploit foreign workers but rather serve to bring the joys of the industrial revolution to less advanced societies. They don't make exorbitant profits. They pay lots of taxes, although not necessarily to the U.S. Government. They don't go seeking low-wage areas for production that can be shipped back to the United States; rather, these companies primarily invest in foreign lands to meet market demands that cannot be served by exports from the United States.

How can you get mad at companies like that? Furthermore, the multinationals see themselves as a first line of defense against selfish nationalism.

A 1973 study conducted by the Emergency Committee for American Trade, a group composed of top executives of the major U.S. multinationals, concluded that a continuing attack on multinational corporations could lead to a renewal of economic nationalism and called for help:

It is the responsibility of every American to see that this does not happen. The multinational company must be treated for what it is, a modern and flexible means for providing the goods and services people need, both in America and in the world.

It seems to me that if the industrial society is worth preserving and expanding, and I'm by no means sure that it is, the multinational corporation is as good a vehicle as any to spread it around. As international business grows and national interests become linked with the well-being of other nations, it could help keep the peace. Would the Japanese have bombed Pearl Harbor if the area contained three Toyota factories, large Sony warehousing facilities, a regional headquarters of Matsushita Electric Industries and a string of Benihana of Tokyo restaurants? World-citizen movements flop because there's no money in them, but the multinationals have found a formula to spread internationalism and make a profit at the same time. It just might work.

While the multinationals were working up studies to polish up their public image, businessmen, bankers and professors were searching for a new monetary system. In July of 1973, a group of blue-chip businessmen, with the advice of the nation's leading monetary experts, issued a report outlining the kind of system they would like to see. The report, by the Research and Policy Committee of the Committee for Economic Development, called for a world economy free of "uncoordinated national controls and restrictions on trade and capital movements"; floating rates with some but not too much central-bank intervention or a fixed-rate, par-value system with frequent small adjustments (it was felt that in substance there was little difference between managed floats and frequently adjusted par-value systems); a stronger role for Special Drawing Rights and the creation of a new lending facility within the International Monetary Fund strong enough to cope with massive movements of funds that might upset exchange markets.

The subcommittee on monetary reform was chaired by Howard C. Petersen, chairman of the Fidelity Bank, Philadelphia, with Kermit Gordon, president of the Brookings Institution in Washington, as co-chairman. Among the expert advisers to the group were C. Fred Bergsten of Brookings; Richard N. Cooper, Henry C. Wallich and William J. Fellner of Yale; Arnold Harberger of the University of Chicago; Peter B. Kenen of Princeton; Charles P. Kindleberger of Massachusetts Institute of Technology and Roy Blough, Columbia University.

Gabriel Hauge, head of New York's Manufacturers Hanover Trust Company, a subcommittee member, took mild exception to the failure of the report to come out unequivocally for a par-value system. He said that while there may not be much difference in practice between a par-value and a floating system under agreed rules, he felt that a par-value system "would be easier to define and administer" and would lend greater encouragement "to the pursuit of sensible domestic policies."

One key recommendation of the report was the use of specific objective indicators—such as the level of reserves—to trigger exchange-rate adjustments. However, the report fell short of recommending automatic action based on changes in objective indicators. Instead the committee recommended international consideration of the need for exchange-rate adjustments when the warning lights flashed.

In the spring of 1974, the Committee of 20, a group of IMF

member nations organized to negotiate monetary reform, came up with the outlines of an agreement. The accord basically set up guidelines for managed floating of currencies and provided an international code of good conduct for central banks. Floats were to be managed, and values were to be kept within an agreed-upon zone. Central banks would be charged with the responsibility of keeping the floating clean by recognizing that there are times when the market may be a better judge of a currency's worth than central-bank officials.

If the world continues moving forward toward greater cooperation and each nation is willing to give up a little of its sovereignty for the greater good, we may come out of this thing whole. Special Drawing Rights or perhaps similar international money with a catchier name will gradually take over the functions formerly filled by gold and dollars. But it won't be an easy transition.

Professor Kindleberger, in a lecture delivered in early 1974, explained some of the difficulties and provided his formula for progress:

> Few are any longer beguiled by gold as the French used to be and few believe that the dollar, the Humpty Dumpty of tomorrow's financial scene, can be put back together again by all the King's Finance Ministers and all his central bankers. Other national currencies such as the Deutschmark, the Swiss Franc and the Yen are shy and unexperienced as international money. Their officials try to keep foreign funds out, rather than welcome them in. . . .

This would leave SDR's, said Professor Kindleberger, as the only alternative. But comparing the dollar and SDR's to two fighters who are so bad that neither can win, he knocks SDR's out of the ring.

> The SDR escapes many of the physical drawbacks of gold, but suffers from the crucial inconvenience that it has to be converted into national money before it can be spent. There are, moreover, many

issues as to how it would be used . . . whether central banks obtaining foreign exchange are obliged to convert it to SDR's, or may hold either asset (thus setting up again the possibilities of Gresham's Law), and especially whether SDR's can be held by the public. If the public cannot hold the SDR, it seems likely that the public will set up another national currency as its own international money, to perform the functions of money. . . .

After much technical analysis covering 24 double-spaced typewritten pages, the good Professor gives his conclusion: "We all bumble along."

V

ECONOMIC FORECASTS

HOW WIDE ARE THE BANDS
ON THE WOOLLY BEARS?

"Economics is extremely useful as a form of employment for economists" is a John Kenneth Galbraithism that is becoming truer all the time.

While the 6-foot-8½-inch Harvard guru of the planned economy and women's liberation was being facetious, his colleagues in the economics business have taken him seriously. The field is growing rapidly and the pay is getting better. Since 1959, as measured by the membership growth of the National Association of Business Economists, the economics industry has grown at an annual rate of 14½ per cent. This compares with an economy that has been growing an average of about 4 per cent a year. If this trend continues, at some point the Gross National Product of the country will come to consist principally of forecasts of next year's Gross National Product.

The professional income of the business economists is also growing at a faster pace than the economy. In 1964, the average business economist earned $18,000 a year. In 1972, the average was $30,000, representing an annual increase of nearly 7 per cent. Thus they will also at some point have nearly all the money.

These forecasts of the ultimate role of the economists are based on the type of reasoning used by economists in their own forecasts, so don't get alarmed. If I had a computer handy I could be more specific and tell you exactly in what year and at what time of day the economists would have taken over the bulk of the Gross National Product and when they would have a lock on the money supply.

On top of normal income channels such as salaries and consulting fees, there's a lucrative lecture circuit available for the economist who has the talent to keep an audience amused or even awake. The fees for appearances before business groups and associations vary widely, depending on the group and the ability of the economist as performer. Some of the big names in the field might pull in as much as $5,000 for a single appearance.

How are lecture fees set? "By good sound economic theory," says one economist. "What the market will bear."

The talks also have a certain public relations value, and a speaking engagement before one group tends to breed calls from other groups.

The best of the showbiz economists is Pierre A. Rinfret, a fifty-year-old French Canadian who holds B.S. and M.B.A. degrees from New York University and a Ph.D. from the University of Dijon in France. Rinfret combines humor with directness and clarity ("There ain't gonna be no recession" is his most famous direct statement. He made it just prior to the 1970 recession), and he's in great demand as a speaker.

He says he used to do 50 appearances or so a year, but decided to cut down to about 24 because of the time they have taken away from his business—Rinfret-Boston Associates, a consulting firm.

Rinfret has also reassessed the impact of his personal appearances, because clients were complaining that while they were paying fat fees for his services (the average client pays $27,000 a year), he was running around the country giving all this information out for nothing. He, of course, does not concede that the information he was "giving away" in his talks in any way diluted the value of the consulting services, but since some clients were unhappy, he decided to cut down. He admits that the audience response and all the publicity fed his ego, but he told me during an interview, "I can't afford that ego kick any more. I'm running an organization."

As economists proliferate, they gain increasing influence on what happens to your money and mine, and that's why I'd like to explore a bit of what they do, how well they do it and whether they should even bother.

The profession is broken up into two major categories. The first is the academic, or "pure," economists, who do basic research and develop techniques for the other category, the business economists, to exploit commercially. There is, of course, much crossing over from one category to the other, so it's sometimes hard to tell the pure from the impure.

Professor Otto Eckstein of Harvard runs an outfit called Data Resources, Inc., which is as slick an economic-consulting business as any Madison Avenue huckster could turn out. Many of the big-name professors—Milton Friedman of the University of Chicago, Walter W. Heller of the University of Minnesota, Paul W. McCracken, University of Michigan, to name a few—do consulting work for commercial firms and also pick up a nice buck on the lecture circuit.

However, there are a host of nameless, faceless economists who do research and teach principles and practices of the dismal science, all the while hoping that lightning will strike and they'll win a Nobel Prize. These are introverted people who would probably be uncomfortable in the plastic jungle of commercial economics. The world of the business economists requires as much salesmanship and showmanship as it does economics.

The successful economic-consulting firm is located in a prestige office building, its quarters decorated in modern good taste. The staff must be cheerful, smiling at all clients or potential clients, and it helps if the girls are attractive. The office must provide an atmosphere of efficient elegance. All reports, graphs and brochures must be done on the highest-quality paper and, where appropriate, bound in clear plastic folders. The ambiance and the product must fairly shout: "Here is an organization that looks to the future, lives in the present but hasn't lost sight of the past."

Although economic forecasting has been equated with everything from witchcraft to prostitution, the forecast is what contemporary economics is all about. Whether it be a "macroeconomic" forecast, which takes in the entire economy, or "microeconomics," which deals with specific companies within the economy, it's forecast or perish in this business.

There have been great strides made in forecasting techniques with computers and economic models and the greater availability of current data. Unfortunately, the improvements in technique have not been matched by the accuracy of the results. The forecasters have had a pretty lousy record in recent years. They missed badly on inflation, which threw just about everything else out of whack, and then they blew the energy crisis.

William McChesney Martin, Jr., former Chairman of the Federal Reserve Board, in February of 1973 expressed disappointment that inflation would not be held to the 2½ per cent hoped for in the year ending June 30, 1974, but rather would surge ahead "in the neighborhood of 4 per cent to 4.5 per cent." Actually, 4 or 4.5 per cent would have been a nice neighborhood, since by the end of 1973 inflation was running at a 10 per cent rate.

Walter W. Heller, 1974 president of the American Economic Association, told the AEA's annual meeting that 1973 was "a year of infamy" for economic forecasters of inflation.

The year 1974 would turn out equally infamous for economic forecasters. In April of 1974 a survey of members of the New York Chapter of the American Statistical Association brought the prediction that the inflationary trend was headed down and that the consumer price index would rise at an annual rate of 6.7 per cent between March and September (it jumped at 14.5 per cent in the first quarter of 1974) and would slow further to a 6.2 per cent rate during the fourth quarter.

Not only have the new techniques failed to solve the central problem, which is looking into the future, but the high technology and advanced mathematics and the arcane language tend to give the forecasts an authenticity they don't deserve.

The computer, with its awesome capabilities, is used to intimidate us. One can take the most complex mathematical formula and program it into one of these monsters and out will come the answer in milliseconds. The answer will be right, but will it make for a better forecast? I doubt it. You can feed a 4.2 per cent compound annual growth rate into a computer and before you know it, the computer will tell you what the Gross National Product is going to be in the year 2000 or even in the year 200,000. But that doesn't make the GNP figure any more valid than if you had painstakingly figured it out with a pencil and paper.

Furthermore, if you had to use paper and pencil, you would think twice to decide if the result would have any real significance before going ahead with some of the complicated calculations. With a computer, you get the figure first and later decide if it's worth anything.

As the owner of a computer that produces all this information, it is in your best interest to find significance in the result and then go out and try to sell it.

Meanwhile, the public is impressed with all those numbers and thinks that computer-based forecasts come down from the mountain. We should recognize the computer for what it is: a data processor. We put the data in, and the computer will spin it around, put it away, bring it back, take the square root of it and spit it back to us. This is of great help in getting airline reservations and calculating the time it would take to get to Mars in a Volkswagen. A computer does not forecast the economy. In fact, it is not unusual for an economist to use a computer for a forecast and, if he doesn't like the answer he gets, ignore it and make up his own.

The nation's best-known computer-based economic model is that of the University of Pennsylvania's Wharton School of Business Administration. Quarterly the Wharton model cranks out its update of the projection for the upcoming quarter and also a one-year and a two-year projection.

Wharton professors, guardians of the econometric soothsayer, hold a press conference, and soon the economic world is made aware of what has been spoken at Philadelphia.

The Wharton School rites strike me as a combination of the ancient Greeks' visits to the Oracle of Delphi for projections on life and the annual trips to the woodlands by "scientists" to measure the bands on the woolly bear caterpillars for a fix on the degree of severity of the upcoming winter.

The major difference is that the Greek oracles never missed, principally because their language was so ambiguous the outcome could always be fitted to the prophecy. In the case of the woolly bears, they have proved almost infallible. The Wharton computer, so far, has proved no better or worse than its human counterparts, and since it's just a dumb machine, it cannot take advantage of the benefits of ambiguity.

The major contribution of the econometric school of economics is that we can now get the wrong answer with lightning speed.

Another quantum leap in the art of economic forecasting is the availability of a wide selection of consensus forecasts. The National Association of Business Economists, the American Statistical Association–National Bureau of Economic Research forecasters panel, the Conference Board and a number of other groups regularly publish consensus forecasts, so the individual practitioner can take his choice.

With the consensus to lean on, economists have become emboldened. You may recall the story about Harry Truman's impatience with his economic advisers. They would tell him that on the one hand the business outlook was pretty bright but on the other hand, there were numerous clouds on the economic horizon. "What I'd like to find," said the President, "is a one-handed economist."

The supply of one-handed economists has increased dramatically since Truman's time. They may not always be right, but with the aid and comfort of so many of their fellow prognosticators out on the same limb, they are willing to stand or fall with their predictions.

Pierre Rinfret, who often finds himself standing alone against the consensus, says preparing a forecast is like solving a whodunit:

> You look for clues everywhere. In statistics, at the trends . . . you look for aberrations. You get input from daily business contacts and you look in everyday experience.
> One of the first clues I noticed that put me on to the inflation that was coming was when my wife came home from shopping for groceries with a package that had the price stamped over three times. Each stamp carried a higher price. That was back in 1966.

So we see forecasts come out of everything from the most sophisticated computer program to the stamp on a can of beans. There is even a school of forecasting called "atmospheric analysis." The technique here is to create a forecast out of thin air.

Adding to the difficulty of making an accurate forecast are the pressures and biases that consciously or unconsciously are programmed into the final judgment. An economist must be influenced by his own position, the company he's speaking for, the school of economic thought he has accepted, just to mention a few of the forces working against a clean forecast. In other words, the economist is not free to make his own mistakes objectively. He may have to decide what kind of projection he *should* make before going ahead with his look into the future.

Take an economist on the President's Council of Economic Advisers. He can't forecast a recession even if every bone in his body tells him that we're going to have one. (The bone-in-the-body school of forecasting is not officially recognized by the National Bureau of Economic Research, but it seems to work reasonably well for economists with minor arthritis pains.)

While one might think it terribly dishonest for an economist to tailor his appraisal of the economic outlook to fit an official party line, he really has no choice. First, he would risk losing a nice cushy job if he decided to deviate. But more important, if government economists were to start predicting a recession, this would virtually ensure that we'd have one.

Businessmen would abandon expansion plans, consumers would stop spending and start burying money in back yards and the entire economy might wind down to a crawl. Conversely, if the Government keeps hammering away at us with lies about how good business is going to be, maybe enough believers will be found to help cushion the shock of the expected recession. This might be called prosperity by proclamation.

Not only must a Government economic spokesman tailor his forecasts; he may even have to adjust his fundamental economic philosophy to fit changing conditions.

Back in 1970 and 1971, Paul McCracken, the Chairman of the President's Council of Economic Advisers, spent a good deal of his time traveling around the country defending the

Administration's "game plan." The plan was to slow down the economy to the point at which unemployment would dampen labor's demands for large wage increases and weakness in sales would cause business to cut prices, or at least limit price increases. The game plan didn't seem to be working and there was a great clamor for price controls, even from business groups. McCracken toured the country and patiently explained that price controls were unworkable, that they just caused distortions in the economy, that President Nixon was philosophically opposed to controls and they just weren't going to happen.

On August 15, 1971, the President froze prices for 90 days and McCracken went on the road to defend this sudden turnabout.

The little professor handled it magnificently. While it was still true that price controls aren't worth a damn, ran the official line, prices were being frozen temporarily mainly for the psychological value. Controls would not have to do anything because underlying economic forces were really holding prices down.

This line was continued into Phase Two of the price-control program when a bureaucracy was put in place to monitor prices and wages. The controls program was working well, said the Administration, because there was no economic need for it.

I have sat through many press briefings, listening to McCracken and then his successor as top economic adviser, Herbert Stein, explain that inflation would soon abate or unemployment would soon peak out and been convinced in my own mind that they didn't believe a word of what they were saying. This would always stir up within me a visceral sense of outrage. But after sober reflection, I'd say to myself: "Stupid, what did you expect them to say? Should they say that inflation will go on forever and that we've lost control of it? Or that unemployment is going to get worse? These people are working for the Government and their job is to keep the economy from coming apart and if a little bending of the truth is required, why not? They're only doing their job."

Furthermore, no economist can be accused of lying about the future, because he doesn't know what the truth is.

Speaking of Government forecasts, J. K. Galbraith, in an article in *New York* magazine, said that they are not forecasts at all but "expressions of the maximally plausible hope."

The same article pointed out, however, that private forecasts are not necessarily better than the Government's.

Many of them [private forecasts] are casual and purely random. A reporter who does not know asks an economist who does not know what he thinks the prospects are for 1972. If the economist says he does not know, the reporter will ask him what economists are for. So he gives an answer. No one holds it against him if he is wrong.

In my own experience, I recall a well-known economist (not Galbraith) expounding at a press conference with great authority on the coming year's GNP and corporate profits and unemployment and the value of the dollar in international markets and the rest of the major indicators of economic well-being. Questions from the newsmen were precise and the answers crisp and unequivocal.

When the conference was over and we were relaxing over our Scotches and Bloody Marys, the Great Man approached one of the hacks in the financial press corps, tugged on his sleeve and with all the confidence drained from his voice, whispered furtively, "What do you think?"

I was so embarrassed at having eavesdropped that I didn't wait around for the answer.

Getting back to Dr. Galbraith's article, he seems to have been taken in by the econometricians, noting that at some point the "more comprehensive efforts of the nongovernmental economists" will be taken seriously. He cites the com-

puter models developed by the Brookings Institution and the
Wharton School, among others, which use "a large amount
of information in a rigorously unemotional fashion." He does
caution that judgment is still involved in feeding these
models.

But even bad forecasts are of use to business.

"It is good to have good forecasts. But without some forecasts there can be no planning at all. And planning based on
bad figures (which can usually be revised) is greatly superior to none at all," Galbraith concludes.

Having given the professional equal time, I'll get back to
explaining how useless and distorted economic forecasts
really are.

The first basic bias in any forecast, after adjusting for outside pressures that have nothing to do with the subject of
economics, is the school the particular economist belongs to.
Of the 415 economists participating in the 1973–74 forecasting survey of the National Association of Business Economists, 57.6 per cent classified themselves as "eclectic judgmental"—which means anything from bone-in-the-body
analysis to a balance of monetarist, Keynesian and econometric methodology; about 10 per cent classified themselves as
straight monetarists; 21 per cent fell into the category of
"eclectic econometric," which is very difficult to say without
bruising your upper palate; and another 10 per cent were
classified as "other" and "no response."

With so many different approaches to economic analysis,
emphasis will vary and the resultant forecast must be
influenced.

The same development will create differing responses in
an economist as a result of his conditioning. Most economists
are so locked into their own little cubbyholes that on Judgment Day the monetarists will still be worrying about its impact on the money supply, the Keynesians will be recommending a tax cut and the free marketers will denounce the

whole affair as a plot to take our freedom of choice away. Who needs Paradise with gold at $200 an ounce?

After a forecast has been grossly misshaped by dogma, the next blow to objectivity comes from the economist's position. The private economist must look at his employer or his biggest clients and decide what they would like to hear before coming up with a firm forecast.

Suppose you're an economist for a brokerage firm. You look at your statistical series, you scrutinize your leading indicators, you analyze all the basic forces at work and then you come up with a forecast that says slow growth and lower corporate profits. Your employer sells stocks and bonds, and periods of slow growth and falling profits make for sluggish turnover in the securities business, and this will make your employer unhappy.

Since you're not sure of your forecast anyhow and a "judgmental" factor is needed to supplement the statistics, why not shade your prediction and make the boss happy? This may seem pretty dumb since you were hired for your economic expertise and guidance. But in the real world, or as close to the real world as the brokerage business is, the economist is usually the first guy to get fired when business is bad, so you'd have nothing to lose by playing the game. If business turns out to be good, you're a hero and you'll get a big raise. If business is bad, you're out of a job regardless of your forecast.

I know of one economist who was fired because he was bearish and his firm was bullish. The economist turned out to be right and smiled all the way to the unemployment office. There are also rumors in financial circles that the economic-consulting arm of one of the big brokerage firms has to clear forecasts with the parent before sending them out. It wouldn't do for a bullish parent to have to operate within a bearish economic forecast.

A classic illustration of the wish being father to the fore-

cast came over my desk from a brokerage firm in May of
1973. The stock market had been falling steadily from the
peaks early in the year, and the generally accepted reason
for the weakness was inflation. Accelerating inflation
spawned high interest rates and tight money and lower stock
prices.

Ahead, said the report, was a period of "disinflation," and
now is the time to buy "relatively low price-earnings multiple, high-quality industrial and utility equities at historically low rates."

The firm noted that although the headlines showed prices
rising at historically high rates, "we have reason to believe
that inflationary pressures will ease over the next few
months."

The prediction was backed with an impressive discussion
of monetary aggregates, a fancy formula and visual aids
(graphs). Inflation was correlated with changes in the
money supply and industrial production, and the figures suggested that the economy was headed for a period when there
would be "too many goods chasing too few dollars."

As it turned out, inflation continued to accelerate through
the summer, and in October the oil embargo came along and
whatever "reason to believe" the brokerage firm had for "disinflation" became inoperative.

A funny thing, though. The economy didn't disinflate, but
the market did come back from the levels of the spring of
1973, and investors who followed the advice to buy low-
multiple industrial stocks could have come out very well—if
they sold on time.

Economists, incidentally, are always coming up with new
words to ensure that the proper atmosphere of mystery and
erudition surrounds their pseudo science. Thus are born
words like "disinflation" and more recently, "compression."
A compression is like a recession except that it is caused by
supply shortages rather than the lack of demand that has

been blamed for previous recessions. In 1974 the economy had its first compression, and to everyone save the economists, it felt just like a recession.

Another example of a forecast that should have been whistled in the dark instead of published was put out by the New York Stock Exchange in October of 1973. It was a period of soft stock prices and low volume. The Big Board issued the results of a survey of 46 economists showing that 95 per cent of them expected stock prices to go up in 1974 and 5 per cent expected prices to remain level.

"Not a single vote was cast in expectation of a market decline next year," said Dr. William C. Freund, the NYSE's chief economist, in a press release accompanying the survey.

A majority of the economists also predicted an easing of inflation and an increase in the average daily volume on the New York Stock Exchange to 17 million shares, up smartly from the 15 million rate at the time of the survey. (By mid-1974 volume was actually running at a 12 million rate and in the first 9 months of the year the Standard & Poor's 500-stock index plummeted 32.7 per cent.)

While I'm not accusing the economists of coming up with a fixed forecast, I'm naturally suspicious of unanimity among a group about which it is said, "Put eight economists in one room and you're sure to get nine opinions." I think that (unconsciously) the respondents were telling the Exchange what it wanted to hear. Since stock prices are impossible to predict anyhow, why not give the New York Stock Exchange and its member firms a little sorely needed comfort?

Assuming an economist can overcome the temptation to please his constituency and the overdependence on a particular economic doctrine, he still must contend with the economics of being an economist. An economist working by himself can't possibly go over all the relevant data required to come up with a solidly based forecast. Chase Econometric Associates, Inc., a subsidiary of the Chase Manhattan Bank, boasts that its data base contains more than 8,500 time series on a monthly, quarterly and annual basis. That's a lot of numbers for an individual practitioner to have to deal with. So he must take short cuts ranging from using statistical services to using other economists' prognostications.

Another disturbing element in the forecasting business is the complete lack of standards for qualifying economists. While most have degrees stretching from one end of the office wall to the other, there is no requirement that an economist have any particular training. If you have a card printed up that says "economist," or you can get someone to hire you as an economist, that's it. As a result, there are people running around making forecasts and holding themselves out as economists whose principal qualifications are a passing acquaintance with the terminology and an outsized portion of *chutzpah*.

In the academic community the pressures are not the same as those bearing on a consulting economist who has to meet a payroll every week or a business economist who has to hold on to his job. But the scholars have their own problems. They are still tied to a pet theory, whether it be Milton Friedman's University of Chicago monetarist free-market school or Walter Heller's Keynesian fine-tuning, pump-priming, activist school.

Also, the academics, with the notable exception of Messrs. Friedman, Heller, Galbraith et al., tend to isolate themselves from the mainstream of business life. They don't have the contacts with the high-powered business executives who are right in the middle of the action. Business economists, particularly the consultants with clients among the largest corporations, have hundreds of meetings with top business executives, and the information they get can be extremely helpful in forecasting.

When sales of machine tools start to slip, for instance, a consulting economist with six or seven clients in the field will know about it quickly and be able to adjust his thinking. Meanwhile, back at the universities, the professors are working with last week's statistics and official Government information that could be outdated before it gets to them.

Morality is another element that can color a forecast. Someone opposed to the use of alcohol may resist indications that there's going to be a huge expansion in beer consumption. An economist who thinks gold has no value outside of dentistry or jewelry will find it difficult to predict a major increase in the price of gold or the re-emergence of gold as the basis for the world monetary system.

The practitioners deny any prejudice based on morality. Pierre Rinfret says he clearly separates the economist from the human being in him. "As a human being," he said, "I would hate to see a depression. As an economist I don't give a damn as long as I had forecast it."

Roy E. Moor, a former president of the National Association of Business Economists, recognized the humanity of economists and in a talk before the group warned against letting it interfere with their jobs:

One of the irrelevant variables in all business analysis is the hope or desires of the individual economist. Wishing never makes it so. Economists in business must learn how to eliminate from their analytical processes their personal value judgments of what should occur. Business economists earn their living by the quality of their analysis, not by the quality of their aspirations. Predictions cannot be based on predilections.

Moor then went on to assure his audience that business wants to know the unvarnished truth:

I am continually impressed, incidentally, by the recognition of this point by American business management. Apparently almost without exception, management want from their economists the most objective results rather than the most pleasant or favorable results.

I am impressed by the feeling that if management really wanted objectivity, the economists wouldn't have to be reminded so often to give it to them.

The basic function of the business economist, in the words of Mr. Moor, is "establishing conceptual bridges between the macro economic environment and the micro economic entity for which they work." This sounds much more scientific than forecasting, but when you pull apart the rhetoric it comes out to using the outlook for the economy as a whole to help an individual company make money. The business economist has to make macro forecasts and break them down into micro forecasts.

Conceptual bridges can be fun to build, but the businessman wants something less esoteric. He wants the economist to plot out the business environment in which the corporation will be operating—inflation, international money conditions, corporate profits, competition, interest rates. He wants to know what his costs are going to be and what his prices should be. Whether he should be in dollars, yen or marks; should he do his long-term borrowing now or wait until interest rates come down? For this kind of information the businessman is willing to pay handsomely, and does. That's the micro part of the economists' analysis, and the quality of information being fed to corporate America must vary from one micro to another. But the record of macro projections has been spread before the public, and the record is none too good.

Economists' record for predicting the stock market has been no more successful than that of any other group, which is to say it's been rotten. The only foolproof system for calling the market is to take a position—bullish or bearish—and keep it for years and years until the market comes your way. You may be wrong a lot, but at least you're assured of being right sometimes, and that's one up on most market experts.

Economists have had so little success with the market that

the National Association of Business Economists dropped the stock-price question from its 1973–74 survey. NABE President Robert G. Dederick, economist for the Northern Trust Company, in telling the group about the results for the prior year in picking the level of the Dow Jones Industrial Average, said:

> You told us that it would be a not unhandsome 1000 at the end of the second quarter. It wasn't. Instead it was a distinctly unattractive 894. Little wonder that most of you aren't rich; and little wonder that I kindly omitted a stock market variable from this year's survey.

Picking the Dow Jones was always treated as a kind of joke by economists, but inflation is no joke, and they have goofed monumentally in recent years.

For 1969, the NABE consensus predicted an increase in the consumer price index of 3.3 per cent, while the actual increase came to more than 5 per cent. The NABE consensus underestimated inflation for 1970 and again for 1971, coming in on target only in 1972, primarily because mandatory price controls kept prices down artificially. For 1973, the combination of voluntary or non–price controls and the impact of skyrocketing fuel prices threw the forecasts into a statistical garbage heap. The consensus predicted a 3.5 per cent rise in the consumer price index. It actually jumped 9 per cent that year, or 157 per cent higher than the prediction.

The record on estimating the Gross National Product has been much better than the inflation fiasco. The 1969 figure was off by a matter of $24 billion, but over-all, the consensus has come in close to the actual figure. However, without a firm grip on the inflation factor, the GNP figure loses much of its significance. What good is a 7 per cent growth in GNP if inflation is in double digits? Also, the economists themselves agree that inflation is the nation's primary economic problem and it must be at the heart of any projection.

Morgan Guaranty Trust Company, in its monthly survey

for December of 1973, pointed out that economists had flopped in their 1973 projections because they had failed to spot the resurgence of inflation and that projections for 1974 "rest on much flimsier foundations than usual" because of the unpredictability of changes consumers will make in their buying habits as a result of the energy situation.

"However diligently one works at building assumptions about switches from bigger to smaller cars, about diminished travel, and about a host of other possible shifts in the pattern of consumer spending, there just can be no confidence that errors in that type of guesstimating won't be substantial," Morgan Guaranty cautioned.

The monetarists at First National City Bank were also extremely cautious about predictions for 1974. In addition to the assortment of unknowns created by the energy crisis, Citibank found in its Economic Week of February 25, 1974, that even the old reliable money-supply-growth forecasting tool had a crack in it. Said Citibank, analysts "must deal for the first time in postwar experience with a policy of money supply growth which is moderately expansive in nominal terms but highly restrictive in real terms, due to the unprecedentedly high rates of inflation."

And a monetarist who can't trust the money-supply figures will write his forecasts in a very shaky hand.

But no matter how uncertain the outlook, the forecasters will not be deterred. They will continue to predict and continue to err. Peter Bernstein, an economic consultant, conceded in the pages of *The New York Times* in the fall of 1973 that economic forecasters had rotten records, but he urged them to hang in there.

The reason forecasters flop, he said with tongue slightly in cheek, is that they fail "to take into account one or another of the few basic, virtually immutable principles that all good forecasts must employ." His first principle was "never believe anyone on the Government's payroll." His final principle: the number of disaster-mongers will always exceed the number of disasters.

One method aimed at avoiding an overabundance of disasters and adding substance to an atmospheric forecast, is to take a poll and ask people about their plans. It doesn't work much better than old-fashioned guessing, but it does impress the clients.

Capital-spending plans of business are polled constantly, because dollars spent on plant expansion and modernization are supposed to have a powerful impact on the rest of the economy—the so-called multiplier effect. Money spent for expansion is multiplied as it moves through the economy, while a slowdown in the capital-goods area is bad news for the rest of the economy.

The Commerce Department makes several surveys of spending plans every year. McGraw-Hill conducts its own, Rinfret-Boston Associates does it and who knows how many other private surveys are taken. However, the survey results for 1974 spending plans wouldn't sit still. In October of 1973, Rinfret-Boston's survey showed plant and equipment spending rising 15.3 per cent in 1974. The next month McGraw-Hill came out with an expected increase of 14 per cent, and in January of 1974 the Department of Commerce, considered the most reliable, came up with a 12 per cent increase. These figures would indicate to the prudent man that capital-spending plans for 1974 were slipping.

Rinfret-Boston reported to its clients that it was disturbed by the trend because it was reminiscent of the pattern that preceded the 1970 recession. The consulting firm decided to resurvey its sample—a group that accounts for 55 per cent of all domestic capital spending.

The new survey generated a figure showing that industry planned to spend $119.4 billion on new plant and equipment in 1974, an increase of 19.3 per cent over 1973.

Whereupon the analysis at Rinfret-Boston tossed aside the

results of the survey and decided that capital spending would be ahead somewhere between 12 and 15 per cent. It seems that the Rinfret-Boston people chose the lower figure "because we do not think there is enough capacity to permit a 19 per cent increase in capital investments in 1974."

Surveys are very helpful as long as the results don't interfere with an economist's preconceptions.

One of the most intriguing surveys in my memory was one taken by Albert Sindlinger & Company, back in August of 1971, which was credited with swinging President Nixon over to the price-controls camp after he had stubbornly resisted in the face of rising inflation.

Federal Reserve Board Chairman Arthur Burns had been pushing for an incomes policy of some kind, and prominent business leaders were calling for controls, but talk in Washington was that the Sindlinger poll, showing consumer confidence at an alarming low, pushed the President over to controls.

Mr. Sindlinger himself, whose original training in poll taking goes back to vaudeville days when he would check the house to determine which acts the customers preferred, appeared as a speaker at a luncheon meeting of the New York Society of Security Analysts to tell about his poll.

The Sindlinger organization's sample for the week prior to August 15 (the day Nixon went on television and announced a sixty-day price freeze along with a number of other dramatic moves in the international monetary field) consisted of a total of 1,231 random telephone contacts projected to represent 109,492,000 households. For the week following the dramatic announcements, the Sindlinger sample was even smaller—1,122 telephone contacts projected to represent this same 109 million–plus households.

What intrigued me about the whole affair was the thought that this economic decision of monumental importance to both this nation and the world might have been based on information supplied by a little over 1,000 people answering their telephones and correlated by a man who had studied economics under Smith & Dale.

Getting back to the business of forecasting, some economists try to distinguish between forecasts and projections, but the difference is largely semantic. A forecast covers a quarter or a year or even two years, but beyond that you've got a projection, and there has been no shortage of such exercises in hyperopia.

If you have a minute I'll tell you what the Gross National Product is going to be in 1982 and what it's going to be in 1990, and if you're still interested, I'll tell you what the economy is going to be like in the year 2000. All this on the best of authority.

For the short range (1982), the General Electric Company's econometric Mapcast service has it all figured out in its *Quarterly Review* issued in January of 1972. The Gross National Product will be up to $2.5 trillion ($2.4846 trillion, to be precise) in 1982. With just two years under the bridge since the projection was made, the GNP estimate for 1973 was already off by about $47 billion. The error can be traced to an inflation rate much higher than GEs economists—or anybody else's for that matter—ever dreamed would appear.

There are other encouraging figures in GE's look into the future, and hopefully they'll stand up better than the GNP estimates. Personal disposable income in 1982 will be up to $894.2 billion, compared with $550.7 billion in 1971. These figures are in 1958 dollars, so they would represent real buying power, not a lot of inflated money.

GE is also optimistic about employment. Its computer sees the unemployment rate holding steady in the 5 to 6 per cent area and then dropping down to 4.3 per cent at the end of the decade.

Looking farther ahead, it's just a short trip to 1990. In February of 1972, at the invitation of President Nixon, the nation's brightest lights from industry, finance and academia gathered in Washington for a White House Conference on the Industrial World Ahead. There were 47 speakers and a barrage of technical papers all focused on the state of the economy in the year 1990.

It was a veritable orgy of Harvard Business School bullshit—functional-performance enterprises, technological and institutional innovation, interactions among technological and nontechnological social-economic parameters and much more. The energy crisis that would hit in 1973 was hardly given a passing mention.

Looking through the papers submitted and condensations of discussions, one might find a vague awareness that perhaps resources are being spent too rapidly and an oil shortage could be a problem, but the emphasis was elsewhere.

It would be impossible to estimate the cost in man-hours, computer time and natural resources wasted in this public relations extravaganza. The paper alone could probably have covered the earth with an 18-inch layer of confetti.

In summarizing the results of the conference, Maurice H. Stans, the Secretary of Commerce, said that by 1990 the United States could save a Gross National Product of nearly $2.5 trillion.

(This may sound a bit conservative, since GE had promised us $2.5 trillion by 1982 and here these experts had us waiting until 1990. The explanation lies in the kind of dollars discussed. The 1990 projection used 1971 dollars, while GE was talking about 1982 dollars blown up by inflation.)

Mr. Stans' summary also held out the expectation of a 36-hour workweek, annual income of over $15,000 for 60 per cent of American families and home ownership for six of every seven families.

There were a lot of other wonderful prospects in store for the American over the coming decades, none of which had to do with resource shortages. Not only didn't these people have the clairvoyance to see into 1990, they didn't even know what their short-term problems were.

Mr. Stans went on about the environment, the disaffection of the young, the friction between labor and management and the lack of understanding by the public of the dimensions and the benefits to the public welfare of high corporate profits.

The Watergate scandal; the indictment of this same Maurice Stans on perjury and conspiracy charges arising out of the financing of President Nixon's 1972 campaign (Stans was acquitted); the Arab oil embargo of October 1973—these were the variables that should have been factored into any formula presuming to tell us about 1990. But in February, 1972, nobody knew about these shattering events as the predictors plunged bravely ahead with their forecasts.

The basic paper on the economy was submitted by The Conference Board, a business-oriented research organization. The Conference Board paper gave Mr. Stans his $2.5 trillion GNP and his 36-hour workweek. The projection also had good news about unemployment in 1990, getting it down to 4 per cent.

On the matter of energy, the paper expressed confidence that the problem would work itself out. Speaking of resources generally, the board said that for the period covered by the projection, "market forces and appropriate public actions will ensure a sufficient supply of resources."

Focusing on energy, it said that total consumptions would not increase as rapidly as the Gross National Product; the underlying assumption was:

the present conventional energy system will continue with "normal" improvements in efficiency and with interfuel competition and substitution within evolving energy markets; and it is assumed that technological gains in the use of fossil fuels will offset the effects of any restrictive regulations aimed at controlling environmental pollution.

The language of the economist appears designed to obfuscate rather than communicate, but after several readings of the above, it appears the Conference Board is telling us that the market place will see that we get the fuel we need for that $2.5 trillion economy and environmental problems will be solved with science.

In a paper specifically dealing with natural resources, Dr. Joseph L. Fisher, president of Resources for the Future, Inc., of Washington, D.C., estimated that the need for petroleum would "nearly double" by 1990, but so would requirements for copper, iron, lead, coal and wood. There was no particular emphasis on oil or energy, for that matter. The main thrust of the paper was pollution control, the hottest issue of the time.

Less than two years after this meeting, pollution control and other environmental issues were put on the back burner. The Alaskan oil pipeline got the go-ahead over the objection of environmentalists, and air-dirtying coal was making a comeback because of the scarcity and high price of oil.

With 1990 safely tucked away, we can now move on to the year 2000 with the aid of Research Institute of America, a New York–based private consulting firm. In 1970 the company put out a report entitled "The U.S. Business Climate. A Three Decade Look Ahead."

The study carefully points out that one of the fallacies to be avoided in projecting the future is to assume that tomorrow's economy is an image of today's, only bigger.

It then goes on to project the Gross National Product at $3.43 trillion in the year 2000, with per capita income rising to $11,200 from $4,780 in 1970. These projections, by the way, are in 1970 dollars, so the projections represent real growth after adjustment for inflation.

In explaining the bullish projection, RIA says that it didn't pull those figures out of the air. It points out that it merely used a 4.2 per cent annual growth rate and notes that the United States did better than that on average in the decade of the 1960's.

"Therefore, RIA is not projecting an extraordinary economic performance, but only one that maintains a recently established pattern."

What was that about not projecting tomorrow's economy in the image of today's, only bigger?

Going back to Dr. Galbraith's notion that even bad forecasts are better than no forecasts, I think he's right so long as the forecasters and the world at large are kept ever conscious of the limitations of these guesstimates of the future. Manufacturers Hanover Trust Company, one of New York City's major banks, prefaces some of its forecasts with a refreshing touch of humility. "A reasonable probability is the only certainty" is the quotation atop the bank's flow-of-funds forecast for 1973.

That little truism stood up infinitely better than the forecast, as the bank underestimated the demand for funds by around $26 billion.

Stung by the fickle finger of financial forecasting, the bank's 1974 projection was even more carefully hedged. "Only when we know little do we know anything; Doubt grows with knowledge," said Manufacturers Hanover, quoting the German poet Johann Wolfgang Goethe.

The culprits in setting agley the best-laid plans of mice and men and economists are known in econometric circles as exogenous variables. And no computer in the world will ever have the capacity to operate effectively in the exogenous zone.

VI

THE STOCK MARKET

INSTITUTIONALIZING DISASTER

The professionals have driven the amateurs out of Wall Street. The share of trading volume attributable to banks, insurance companies, mutual funds, pension funds and other guardians of OPM (other people's money) has expanded dramatically, and by 1974 institutions were responsible for about 70 per cent of the trading on the New York Stock Exchange.

Institutions also increased their holdings of NYSE shares tremendously in the postwar period. In 1949, these professionals held $11.1 billion in NYSE-listed stocks, or 14.5 per cent of the total. By 1973 this had shot up to $226.2 billion, or 31.4 per cent of the $721 billion worth of stock listed on the Big Board. And that's not all. The NYSE concedes that there are institutional holdings not readily identifiable and if these were included, the institutional share of all NYSE stocks in 1973 would be in the neighborhood of 45 per cent.

With an institutional market, we have seen a new wave of sophistications in the management of money. We have seen airline stocks all tailspin together because a couple of mutual-fund managers decided to dump their holdings. We've seen stocks fall 20 or 30 points in one day because earnings were flat in a single quarter and the institutional boys were afraid that another growth stock was about to become cyclical. We've seen the computer used to pour out miles of useless information, working out complicated formulas in which the results match the accuracy of the questionable estimates fed into the machine in the first place.

In short, we've seen the professionals dazzle the individual investor with pseudo sophistication, with betas and alphas and gammas and promises of superior performance based on professional management. These promises have not been fulfilled, and the individual has been driven from the stock market.

But the stock market is too good a thing to be left to the professionals, and ultimately common sense will overcome. The market will come back, and so will the individual investor. Gold coins, antiques or Swiss bank accounts may serve as bomb shelters during periods of panic, but who wants to live in a bomb shelter? The real producers of real wealth are corporations grinding out goods and performing services and earning profits, and common stocks provide a reasonable vehicle for sharing in those profits.

There is no way to reduce stock-price movements to a neat mathematical formula. All the intelligent stock-market investor can do is try to analyze the forces at work in general terms, estimate the permanency of these forces, guess the future and what the market will pay for these developments, learn the salient features of various types of investments available—and then put his money down and watch the dice roll.

One attempt by a computer service to sell the Wall Street community on a formula for figuring the market mathematically stands out in my mind as typical of the triumph of technology over common sense.

This group came down to Wall Street to a luncheon of the New York Society of Security Analysts to explain how it had worked out a formula for forecasting the sales and earnings of any given company. Now, this is not quite as good a formula for forecasting the price of stock, but knowing what sales and earnings are going to be would be extremely helpful in gauging future price action.

There was a slide presentation, and the formula, which was full of coefficients and all the other tools of the mathematician's trade, ran the full length of the screen. But it boiled down to something like this: forecast the Gross National Product, estimate the percentage of the GNP the particular industry the given company was in accounted for, then put in the percentage of the industry the company represented and add several other forecasts, any one of which would be as difficult to estimate as the future sales and profits of the company you're dealing with.

The best parallel to this type of thinking was that of the old farmer who had come up with a simple way of keeping track of how many sheep he had: he just counted the legs and divided by four.

The New York Stock Exchange has developed a model for forecasting daily trading volume. It runs as long as your arm and is a most impressive mathematical accomplishment. But there's a problem. One of the key inputs is a projection of the change in stock prices over the period you're trying to forecast. Given a choice between trying to forecast stock prices and trying to predict average volume, I'd much rather try my hand at the latter.

I should say that I think all these mathematical models serve a useful purpose in establishing relationships among a number of variables.

But the number of variables that go into the price of a stock are infinite, and while I wouldn't want to be accused of standing in the way of progress, I do think the mathematicians should be aware of what they're up against. We know the current price and how the stock has acted in the past, but after that we're flying blind.

Will there be peace or war? Will some judge decide to grant a multimillion-dollar judgment against the company? Will another company decide to sue your company? Will the Government follow a loose or tight money policy? Will the President resign and leave the country in the hands of an unknown quantity? Will the President not resign and leave the country in the hands of a known incompetent? Will the French float the franc or the Japanese upvalue the yen? Will the Arabs turn off the oil? Will your company suddenly have a flat quarter in earnings? Will there be a shortage of copper? Will there be a surplus of soybeans? Will *The Wall Street Journal* print a story about insiders' selling stock in your company?

Will *Barron's* challenge the accounting practices of your company? Will your company challenge the accounting practice of *Barron's*? Will Merrill Lynch, Pierce, Fenner & Smith put out a Buy recommendation on your selection? Will A. G. Becker put out a Sell recommendation?

The answers to all those questions and heaven knows how many others all go into determining the market price of a stock. We may develop a computer that can walk, talk and whistle "Dixie" in twelve languages, but it ain't going to be able to forecast the stock market.

Conceding that the market can't be figured with any degree of accuracy or consistency doesn't mean we should give up and get out. It's still the best game in town and, when it is working properly, serves a vital economic purpose.

Members of the Wall Street establishment see themselves as suppliers of capital for industry, the lifeblood of the economy. They see Wall Street as a great center for garnering the savings of millions and channeling the money into the most productive areas.

The stocks listed on major exchanges or traded over the counter don't raise capital for industry. This is a secondary market, and the seller gets paid by the buyer, the broker gets his piece and the company whose stock is being traded is just a passive third party whose principal function is to see that the bookkeeping is taken care of to reflect who the shareholders are at any particular time.

But the market does serve as a pricing mechanism for new issues of stocks and bonds that do raise capital for industry. Thus if a corporation is selling on an exchange at $50 a share and the corporation needs more money, it's possible to sell new shares to the public, and the $50 price will serve as a guide in pricing the new issue.

Likewise, if a company has no stock in the hands of the public, the underwriter will use the market price of similar companies as a pricing guide. The price of stock is measured in terms of earnings. A $50 stock that earns $5 a share is selling at ten times earnings and is cheaper than a $25 stock that is earning $1 a share and thus selling at twenty-five times earnings.

This price/earnings-ratio concept is at the heart of stock values and has become the status symbol for corporate America. A high P/E is better than money in the bank, because it means you are getting more for a dollar of your earnings than the fellow with a low P/E is getting for his. This is particularly important for insiders who may hold large blocks of stock in a company. A change in P/E can make overnight millionaires as well as overnight ex-millionaires.

In any case, without the secondary market there would be great difficulty in floating new issues and raising capital. This was amply illustrated in 1973 when new stock issues were almost impossible to sell because of the depressed condition of stock prices. Stocks were selling at three or four times earnings, and this meant that comparable new issues would sell at those prices or below. Selling new stock under those conditions would be tantamount to giving your business away, and this is not the capitalist way of doing things.

There were only 100 new stock issues in 1973 (compared with 1,026 in the hot-issue year of 1969), and most of them promptly went down in price. According to Arthur Lack, the publisher of *New Issue Outlook*, a computerized statistical service covering the new-issue market, by the end of 1973 prices of the 417 most recent issues had fallen 52 per cent below the average price at which they were originally sold to the public.

The investment-banking function of the securities business has to do with raising capital through selling stock or floating bonds. Investment bankers will price a stock or bond issue and then proceed to try to sell it at that price. If the price is too high, the underwriter will have to absorb the loss.

Underwriting or investment banking is generally a much more profitable business than brokerage, and the fact that new issues dried up was one of the causes for the profit squeeze on Wall Street in 1973 and 1974.

The past five years have been extremely trying for the brokers, the money managers, the underwriters and just about everyone connected with the investment community. The "Little Guy" has withdrawn, disillusioned and depressed, feeling that he's been taken by the "Big Guys."

But the Big Guys in the stock market are principally surrogates of the Little Guys, and the market has been remarkably indiscriminate in its rough handling of the big and little. The mutual-fund industry, for example, lost about $12 billion in 1973. Morgan Guaranty & Trust Company, which managed over $27 billion in trust-fund accounts, the biggest pool of investment funds managed by anyone anywhere, dropped an estimated $5 billion in that one year.

The market also has a way of making today's genius turn into tomorrow's nonentity. Gerald Tsai, Jr., a Shanghai-born money manager, held the hottest hand on Wall Street for a number of years during the 1960's, and his Manhattan Fund was oversubscribed tenfold when it came out. When he was hot, all Wall Street looked to the "Chinaman" for leadership. A Yale professor who was convinced that stocks chosen at random would do as well as stocks chosen by a professional money manager made an exception in his theory when it concerned "a genius like Gerry Tsai." Yet in the space of one year (1968), his fund went from the top of the charts to the bottom, and in February of 1973 Tsai resigned as head of Tsai Management & Research Corporation.

I also recall a money manager whose principal credential was the discovery of Control Data, a young maker of computers whose stock skyrocketed during the go-go days when computer stocks were rising as fast as their little circuits could calculate. Control Data has since settled down to a tame middle age, managing to remain in the black with the help of the profits of a large finance company it acquired. The money manager has likewise faded from the forefront of the investment scene.

Another example of how the professionals are fooled by the market as easily as the rankest of amateurs is furnished by a survey taken by *Institutional Investor,* a trade publication for professional money managers. Of the ten favorite stocks selected by the pros at the beginning of 1973, only one was ahead at year end—Digital Equipment, up $3\frac{3}{8}$ to $101\frac{3}{4}$. Among the big losers: TelePrompTer plunged from $29\frac{3}{4}$ to $3\frac{7}{8}$, and Levitz Furniture collapsed from $21\frac{3}{8}$ to $3\frac{3}{4}$.

So much for the professionals' choices. They don't seem to be any smarter than the rest of us. But amateur or professional, if you play the game, you should know the fundamentals. Wall Street offers a large range of merchandise with varying characteristics, many of them misunderstood.

For instance, there's a widely held belief that high-grade bonds are safer than high-grade common stocks. If you buy a top-rated bond, you're guaranteed a fixed return over the term of the bond and when it matures you get your entire investment back. The only risk the buyer takes is that the company that issues the bond may go bankrupt and default. Top-rated companies rarely go broke; therefore the risk is minimal. Furthermore, even if the company does go broke, the bondholder, as a creditor, will have to be paid before a common stockholder gets anything.

It would appear, then, that all you have to do to keep from losing money in bonds is pick the bond of a company that won't bust.

Not true. The smallest part of the risk in buying a bond is the possibility of default. The real risk in owning bonds is a market risk based on the level of interest rates. There are several insurance companies that are willing to insure municipal bonds against default, but none ready to insure against market risk.

Back in 1946, bonds were paying around 2 per cent interest. If you put up $1,000, you earned $20 a year on your investment. In 1970, long-term bonds were paying 9 per cent, so that same $1,000 invested in new bonds would give you $90 a year. Now, suppose you needed some money and wanted to sell your 2 per cent bond in 1970. You'd have to mark the price of that bond down to the point at which a buyer would be getting 9 per cent on his money. This means that on the basis of yield, that $1,000 bond was worth only about $225 because that would be all you'd have to invest to earn $20 at 9 per cent. There is another factor that goes into the price of a bond and that involves the time to maturity. If a low-interest bond is close to maturity, the price will be higher than the yield implies because at maturity the bond should be paid off at face value. But the point I'm making is that the price of a bond will fluctuate sharply depending on the level of interest rates.

This works both ways. If you bought a $1,000 bond in 1970

that paid 9 per cent and wanted to sell it early in 1974 when the going rate on long-term corporate bonds was 8 per cent, you'd be able to make a profit. Your bond would be marked up to the point at which $90 represented an 8 per cent return. By mid-1974 the profit would have turned to a loss as long-term rates set new highs. When interest rates rise, bond prices drop, and when interest rates fall, bond prices go up.

Trying to forecast the direction of interest rates is as difficult as forecasting the price of a stock. Long-term interest rates tend to move on the basis of supply and demand and on the rate of inflation. Every lender tries to get enough return to cover the depreciation of his money during the period the borrower has the use of it, plus a profit. As the rate of inflation increases, so will long-term interest rates, and my guess is that the long-term trend of interest rates is still upward and bond prices will continue to fall.

In October of 1972, a small fund called Capital Preservation Fund, Inc., was offered to the public with the objective of doing just what the name implies by investing in the bond market. Less than a year later, in August of 1973, the fund sent a letter to its shareholders advising them that the fund's share price had been declining "along with the price declines in the long term bonds in our portfolio."

The letter continued: "We have just sold *all* of the Fund's long term bonds to stop this price erosion. The proceeds were invested in U.S. Government Securities maturing within six months and paying us 9 per cent." Capital Preservation has since been operating as a money-market fund—an inflation-fueled format that will be taken up later in more detail.

Bonds traditionally are issued with "call protection," usually covering a ten-year period from date of issue. The purpose of this feature is to protect the investor against having his bond called if interest rates decline. If a bond has a coupon of 8 per cent and long-term interest rates drop to 6 per cent, the issuer would be tempted to call in the 8 per cent bonds and sell 6 per cent bonds instead. With call protection, he cannot do this without paying a large premium to call the bonds. But this protection in the present economic environment is just more boiler plate. The buyer of bonds needs protection against the probability of rising interest rates, not against the remote possibility that rates will decline.

Another investment supposed to be safer than common stock is preferred stock. It gets its name from the fact that it gets preference in dividend payments over common stock and has a prior right to the assets of the company in liquidation. The order for corporate pay-outs in normal operations gives first priority to interest on bonds; then come dividends on preferred stock and finally, if there is any money left over it goes for dividends on common stock. The same order holds if a company is liquidated. First the creditors, which includes bondholders, are paid; then the owners—preferred and common stockholders—share in the remainder, with preferred holders standing ahead of the holders of common.

On the face of it, bondholders have a safer investment than stockholders, and preferred stockholders have an advantage over common stockholders.

This advantage comes into play only when the issuing corporation is doing poorly or is going to be closed out. In the real world, most major corporations make money and easily cover preferred dividends; they rarely go into liquidation. So the safety in preferred shares is theoretical. In reality, the risk of holding preferred stock is even greater than the market risk in bonds. At least bonds have a maturity date, and if you live long enough, you can eventually recoup your principal. But many preferred shares are open-ended and the issuing corporation can redeem them at its convenience. If a particular preferred issue is paying dividends below the going rate of return on long-term bonds, the corporation just lets it ride. If the return on preferred stock is above the going rate, then the company may decide to call in the shares.

For instance, a $100 preferred share paying a $5 annual dividend would sell at a discount if the going rate for long-term funds was 8 per cent. There would be no economic reason for the issuer, unless required to by the terms of the issue, to redeem the stock. It would be getting a bargain—5 per cent money during a period when the going rate was 8 per cent. But if it should go the other way and the price of long-term money were to drop to 3 per cent, then the company might just go out and borrow to redeem the shares, replacing 5 per cent money with 3 per cent money.

Either way, the preferred stockholder gets shafted.

With municipal bonds, the investor gets stuck tax-free. The interest on municipal bonds is exempt from Federal income tax and, in some cases, state and city taxes. Banks have traditionally been the principal buyers of municipal bonds, and for banks they are not a bad investment. With Federal taxes at nearly 50 per cent for corporations, a 5 per cent return tax-free is equivalent to around 10 per cent taxable. Also, banks carry municipal bond investments on their books at cost rather than market, so a $1,000 bond might have a market value of $500, but the bank can still carry it at $1,000. It would not have to show a loss unless it sold the bond at below face value.

At one point during the 1969–70 credit crunch when interest rates were rising at an alarming rate, the president of one of New York City's largest banks commented (off the record, of course) that if banks were required to carry their municipal-bond portfolios at market value "I think every bank in the country would be insolvent."

Municipal bonds are fine for high-bracketed individuals looking for tax-free income, but there is the ever-present danger to principal posed by rising interest rates.

Default has not been a major problem with municipals.

Even in the depression period from 1929 to 1933, less than 2 per cent of the tax-free issues defaulted, and many of these eventually paid off. This compares with a 6 per cent default rate for utility bonds and 16 per cent for railroad bonds during the same period.

A bank with a municipal-bond portfolio that it has maintained over a long period of time can roll it over as bonds mature and can operate profitably in this market. But an individual who buys a few bonds for income and then finds he needs the principal may sometimes have to take a beating with this "safe" investment.

In the post–World War II years, the trend of interest rates has been upward, threatening to make obsolete any securities that offer a fixed rate of return. One technique for sweetening these issues is to make them convertible into common stock.

The convertible concept caught fire in the 1967–68 period when concepts were all the rage on Wall Street. Here was a sure thing for both the issuer of the security and the buyer. The issuer could borrow money at bargain rates because of the added value given the bond by the convertible feature.

For the investor there was extra protection against rising interest rates. If interest rates kept rising and bond prices dropped, the investor could convert his bond into stock and make money that way. The convertible bond became a popular form of Chinese money used by the acquisition-hungry conglomerates in their corporate empire building.

In the three-year period from 1967 through 1969, there were about $12 billion in convertible bonds issued, according to Salomon Brothers. By 1973, convertibles had lost their charm and only about $400,000 worth were floated.

The declining interest in convertibles stemmed from a financial double whammy. Interest rates went up and stock prices fell simultaneously in 1969–70. This meant that the low-yielding convertibles couldn't compete as bonds, and the conversion price of the stocks was so much above the market price that convertibility became academic.

As an indication of what has happened to convertibles, a major mutual fund picked at random showed ten convertible issues as of October 31, 1973. Only two were selling at above face value. Over-all, the convertibles in the portfolio had a face value of $21 million and a market value of only $17 million.

The fact that bonds, convertible or straight, can sell way below their face value does create an opportunity to profit from someone else's mistakes. Such "discount bonds" sell below par value in the market place not only because of interest-rate changes but also because of varying elements of risk.

Take Pan American World Airways, as an example of extreme-discount bonds. Pan Am has been losing gobs of money, and if it continues along those lines it could go broke and possibly default on its bonds. It may also turn around and be in a position to pay off when the bonds mature.

In early August of 1974, the bond table in *The New York Times* listed seven different issues of Pan Am bonds selling at varying discounts. There were two straight-debt issues originally offering over 11 per cent and four convertibles with coupons ranging from 4½ per cent to 7½ per cent. A Pan Am bond offering 11¼ per cent interest and maturing in 1986 was selling at $680 per $1,000 in face value.

If you think Pan Am is going to make it, you could get over 16.5 per cent current return (the coupon rate is based on the $1,000 face value) plus a chance for capital appreciation of $320 on each bond if you hold to maturity.

On that same August Sunday, the *Times* listed four issues of Rapid American Corporation bonds, also selling at substantial discounts. You could buy a $1,000 Rapid American bond paying 7½ per cent and maturing in 1985 for $500. This would mean a current yield of 15 per cent and the possibility of making $500 on appreciation if you held the bond to maturity.

Unlike Pan Am, Rapid American was making money, but for various reasons, including the flamboyance of its chairman, Meshulam Riklis, the company was regarded as less than top-quality by the Wall Street establishment. Rapid American has had its good years and bad years, but it doesn't appear on the verge of bankruptcy and has a chance of lasting out the next decade. Riklis has stated himself that discount bonds offer a good chance to make money, although his thinking may have been colored by the fact that his company's bonds were so sharply discounted in the market.

When the market price of a bond issue goes way below face value, it is possible for the issuing company to pick up the bonds at a discount by offering less than the face amount in a new issue carrying a higher coupon. This works to almost everybody's advantage. The company is able to reduce its debt and the bondholder will get a higher return. The losers are those who originally bought the bonds at face value or thereabouts. For example, in April of 1974, Fedders Corporation offered $700 in 8⅞ per cent bonds plus $50 in cash for each $1,000 of an old issue of 5 per cent convertibles. Similarly, Chelsea Industries offered $650 in 10 per cent convertibles for $1,000 5¼ per cent convertibles. In each case, the old debentures were selling at sharp discounts in the market.

Some knowledgeable businessmen feel that the return on many of the discount bonds is worth the risk. Reflecting this attitude, a finance-company executive, whose business involves lending money at what many consider outrageous interest rates, was impressed by the return available in these bonds.

"I just bought some discount bonds—Columbia Pictures, at thirty-five," he told me. "At that price I'm getting seventeen per cent on my money and I think the company is going to be all right. But even if it goes broke, I'm sure they'll be able to pay off thirty-five cents on the dollar so I'll get my investment out."

The opportunity for profits in discount bonds has arisen from the fact that new bond issues have proved to be such rotten investments over the years. In the summer of 1974, only 18 out of the 1,000 or so bond issues listed in *The New York Times* were selling at par or above. All the rest of these New York Stock Exchange–traded issues were selling at discounts, with many at less than half their face value.

Bond traders can make money on day-to-day fluctuations, but the long-term investor has been hurt. And if inflation continues as a permanent feature of our economy, there will have to be some changes in the terms under which corporations raise long-term money. A fixed-interest bond doesn't make economic sense in this environment.

Even if inflation doesn't become a fixture and interest rates rise and fall cyclically, a bond with an interest rate that floats up and down with economic conditions is a reasonable alternative. There is simply no justification for either a borrower or a lender to be locked into an unrealistic interest-rate schedule over a 20- or 30-year period.

The importance of interest rates on investments is pointed up in a study by Salomon Brothers, one of Wall Street's biggest investment houses, covering return on different types of securities for the five years for 1969 through 1973. The study found that on average, the best thing an investor could have done with his money during the period was to have kept it in money-market instruments—virtually the equivalent of cash.

Because of the high short-term interest rates available during the period, investments in securities such as certificates of deposit (time deposits) and U.S. Treasury bills yielded a better return than common stocks or long-term bonds. Money-market instruments earned a total return, which takes in interest and capital appreciation or depreciation, of 8 per cent in 1973. In the same year long-term corporates returned 1 per cent, long-term Government bonds yielded nothing and common stocks, as measured by the Standard & Poor's composite index of 500 stocks, lost 15 per cent.

Over the five-year period, money-market instruments returned an average of 7 per cent a year, long-term Government and municipal bonds returned 5 per cent and common stocks yielded an average annual return of only 3 per cent.

Despite this sorry showing for common stocks over those five years, they remain a rational investment for the kind of full-employment, inflation-prone economy I expect.

Over the years, common stocks, as measured by the popular averages, have done much better than bonds. There have been bear markets and bull markets, but each successive high, right through to the beginning of 1973 when the Dow Jones Industrials broke through the 1,000 mark, has been above previous peaks.

Common stocks are risky and some are disaster-prone, but they give the investor a fighting chance. Long-term, fixed-interest-rate bonds and preferred stock are bad news for any investor except those who are willing to sacrifice part of their principal for current yield.

A common stock represents a portion of ownership of a corporation, and if the corporation makes money, the common stockholder is entitled to his share of that profit. He gets it in the form of dividends and in profits reinvested in the business to increase the base for future profits. Common stocks logically provide protection against inflation, and if we ever get a rational market, they will.

But the market that I have been watching for the past decade or so has been so hung up on growth and assorted fads that it has lost sight of reality.

A good part of the blame can be laid at the door of the

market professionals with their tendency to equate jargon with clairvoyance and their willingness to pay more for to-morrow's promise than for today's substance.

They built a market in which a stock that earned 10 cents a share last year, made 20 cents a share this year and prom-ised to make 40 cents next year commanded a much higher price than a company that earned $1 last year, made 90 cents this year and lacked "earnings visibility" for next year.

It wasn't how much a stock earned that mattered, it was compound growth. This mentality also extended to divi-dends, which were virtually ignored. The price/earnings ra-tio became the central measurement of value: how many times earnings did a stock sell for? It made no difference if nothing was paid out. If it paid nothing, all the better, since earnings could be retained for more and faster growth.

VII

THE GROWTH SYNDROME

INVITING MALIGNANCY

There's an old-fashioned theory that the only reason common stocks have any value at all is that they pay dividends or will someday pay dividends. In the interest of growth, this theory was dumped.

What the hell difference did it make if a stock paid dividends or not as long as it was growing 15 per cent compounded annually? If a $10 stock went to $20 in a year, you had a 100 per cent return and dividend or no dividend, nobody gave a damn. The traditional spread between bond and stock yields became an anachronism. Anyone who thought he could call the market by watching dividend rates and interest rates on bonds belonged in a museum.

Let little old ladies worry about dividends. We're aggressive money managers and we'll get you an annual return of 20 per cent or 30 per cent and if we can't, we should be driving cabs and not managing money. After the 1969–70 unpleasantness many of the money managers did go back to driving cabs, and those who still had jobs began to talk of more "realistic" goals—maybe 10 per cent a year, or how about 8 per cent? That's still better than bond portfolios have been yielding.

But as soon as the market started coming back from its low of the spring of 1970, the growth stock returned. But now it was the "quality growth stock" that captivated the professionals. They wanted no more of those plain growth stocks that might suddenly stop growing.

The growth cult ran some stocks up to outrageous prices and at the same time put tremendous pressure on corporations trying to satisfy Wall Street's addiction. The corporations took to creative accounting—holding back on necessary write-offs or changing accounting systems to avoid breaking their beautiful growth patterns. They worked out mergers designed to cover any slowdown in growth rate. Some sought to expand much faster than their capital and management capabilities could support. Some turned to outright fraud.

There was Equity Funding Corporation of America, an insurance company that was called the fastest-growing financial-services firm in the country. Wall Street was so crazy about Equity Funding that at one point it ran its stock up to $81 a share, and the issue was held by a host of major financial institutions.

It maintained its growth image by writing bogus insurance policies and selling them to reinsurers.

The fraud was discovered through the combined work of a Wall Street analyst and a disgruntled Equity Funding executive. Ironically, the analyst who unearthed the massive deception was drummed out of his profession for doing his job too well. He informed his clients that there was something rotten in Century City, Equity Funding's plush Beverly Hills, California, headquarters, before telling the Securities and Exchange Commission and the New York Stock Exchange. It seemed an almost instinctive reaction to punish this brash analyst who had had the bad taste to disturb Wall Street's dream of never-ending growth. (The analyst, Raymond L. Dirks, was grudgingly readmitted after more than a year in exile.)

The Equity Funding fraud involved fake insurance policies with a face value of $2.17 billion, and it took the combined efforts of about 1,000 employees working with computers to hold the scheme together. After the company went into bankruptcy proceedings in 1973, ten months of digging by 50 accountants from the firm of Touche, Ross & Company and an assortment of lawyers and clerks still failed to account for some $80 million in missing cash. A report by the bankruptcy trustee said that the company may have been issuing fraudulent financial statements going back eight years before the bankruptcy and it may never have generated any real profits. The entire company, said the trustee, was "virtually a fiction concocted by certain members of its management." The fiction, the report continued, was "enlarged year by year until EFCA had been proclaimed the fastest-growing diversified financial company in Fortune's list."

In the name of growth, Equity Funding had produced a balance sheet showing a net worth of $143.4 million, when in reality the company had a deficit of $42 million.

Another disaster of the post–go-go years was Levitz Furniture, a chain of furniture stores that had a concept. Here was a store where a buyer didn't have to wait months after placing an order to get delivery. A customer could walk into a Levitz store, pick out the furniture he wanted, put it into the trunk of his car or the back of his station wagon and drive home with it. Beautiful. The idea was an instant success, and the chain began to grow.

Wall Street got wind of it, and Levitz became the growth stock of 1971 and early 1972. To remain a growth stock, a company has to keep getting bigger, preferably at an accelerating pace, and Levitz opened new stores with a passion. And the more stores it opened, the higher its sales were and the happier it made the members of the investment community.

The chain's ten-year growth pattern was an underwriter's dream. From 1964 through the year ended January 31, 1973, sales and earnings charged ahead in great leaps with not one downward blip. In 1964 sales were $3,173,000, and ten years later they were $323,801,000. Earnings per share soared from 1 cent in 1964 to 72 cents in fiscal 1973. If Levitz could continue that pace over the succeeding ten years, by 1982 it would be earning $51.84 a share and sales would be running at about $35 billion. Who could fault a price of $60 a share for a company with prospects like that?

Until the stock went into a dive, the chain maintained a dazzling record of sales increases. For the 11 months to the end of December, 1971, sales were up 82 per cent. The next month the chain showed a sales increase of 97.4 per cent. There was no stopping this company. There was a stock split in 1971, and in 1972 the stock was split 3 for 1. This came just prior to a move by the Securities and Exchange Commission that started the crash.

The SEC questioned some of the financial information that had been dispensed by Levitz, and for a period in the spring of 1972, trading was halted. The SEC matter was settled by agreement, but after trading resumed the stock dropped 24½ points in one week, descending from 59½ to 35. In the fall Levitz lost another 20 points when the head of the company said August earnings figures would be about the same as those of August, 1972. The final blow came with several quarters in which earnings declined and sales gains were fading.

In January of 1974 sales increased by a meager 4.7 per cent, and for the full year the increase was only 16.3 per cent. The stock was selling for about $4 a share. For the year ended January 31, 1974, Levitz earned 51 cents a share, compared with 72 cents in the prior year. Good-bye.

The pressure for growth is almost irresistible once management tastes the blood of a high-flying stock. When Levitz went to the public for more money in May of 1969 (it went public initially July 9, 1968), the stock was sold for $34 a share, bringing the company about $8 million and Levitz family members something over $11 million. After that sale the family still held 1,250,400 shares. Adjusting for splits, the paper value of those holdings at the stock's peak price would have been in the neighborhood of $450 million. Not bad for a family that had started a little furniture store in Pottstown, Pennsylvania, in 1936.

With this kind of astronomical reward for management of a growth company, there's a powerful temptation to take some risks.

And the Levitz family was not alone with its multimillion-dollar paper losses. The financial institutions were also zonked. T. Rowe Price Growth Stock Fund—the largest no-load fund in the business, with assets of better than $1 billion and one of the best long-term growth records among the funds—had invested heavily in Levitz. Toward the end of 1973, the fund closed out 867,000 Levitz shares and lost $24 million on the sale.

The flat-quarter syndrome which helped to wipe out Levitz as a growth company came to be one of the features of the growth hysteria of the 70's. Two of the more notable victims were Simplicity Pattern Company, Inc., and Avon Products.

On February 6, 1974, Simplicity Pattern was a company that had built a reputation as a growth vehicle with an unbroken string of earnings gains going back to 1960, a strong institutional following, three stock splits in ten years, a series of stock dividends and a steadily increasing cash dividend—10 cents in 1962 rising to 31 cents a share in 1972.

On that February day, the company issued a press release that read as follows:

Robert M. Shapiro, President of Simplicity Pattern Co., Inc., reported today that preliminary estimates indicate that Simplicity's fourth quarter operations will reflect a profit of approximately 20 cents a share as against 26 cents in the fourth quarter of last year.

The release went on to report that sales would be down slightly for the quarter and that for the full year earnings would be up to about $1.14 from $1.09. It explained that higher costs and lower sales in the quarter had hurt profit margins and that the sales dip reflected general economic conditions. The company also announced that it had declared a regular quarterly dividend of 8¼ cents a share.

Mr. Shapiro might just as well have stopped right after the first sentence, because nothing he said after that really mattered: 20 cents a share compared with 26 cents last year—that was the whole story.

The next day trading was halted until the orders of panicky sellers and strong-stomached buyers could be matched up and a sale concluded. Finally a block of 100,000 shares was traded at $21 a share, down 11 points from the prior day's closing. Before the session ended, Simplicity Pattern had been down as low as 19 and closed at 20—minus 12 points for the day. The shakeout continued the following day, when Simplicity showed up at the head of the New York Stock Exchange's most-active list with another 2½ points knocked off the price. In two trading sessions, a stock that was rated as "investment grade" by Moody's Investment Service fell from 32 to 17½, a drop of 45.3 per cent. "Investment grade" is Moody's second-highest rating.

By the beginning of March, Simplicity Pattern dipped to 15½ after Mr. Shapiro told a meeting of security analysts that he was not too optimistic about sales and earnings prospects for the immediate future.

Avon Products was another of the more visible victims of the flat-quarter syndrome. Avon's concept was the door-to-door sale of cosmetics, and its growth record was spectacular. From 1958, when it first appeared as a public company, the Avon ladies kept ringing up higher sales and profits—

year after year and quarter by quarter. In 1972, Avon became the first cosmetics company to top $1 billion in sales. There were 240 major financial institutions holding more than 5½ million shares of Avon stock. This was known as "strong institutional support" and served to bolster the price of the stock. Earnings climbed steadily over the years from 19 cents a share in 1958 to $2.16 in 1972.

But the next year, the trouble started. Not that the company wasn't still growing and making lots of money. It was just that there were signs of deceleration.

For the first half of 1973 Avon's earnings were up 14 per cent, but the increase was only 10 per cent in the second quarter, an indication that growth was beginning to taper off. A quarter-by-quarter comparison for all of 1973 showed a gradual tailing off of growth. Per-share earnings were ahead 6 cents in the first quarter, 4 cents in the second quarter and just 2 cents in the third quarter. The fourth quarter, which takes in the all-important Christmas selling season, recorded a gain of 6 cents a share, but that represented an increase of only a bit over 6 per cent—hardly the magnitude needed to sustain a price of about 50 times annual earnings that Avon had come to expect.

In the spring of 1973 Avon stock hit a high of 140, and then it started to topple. By year end it was down to around 100, and in the first quarter of 1974 the stock fell all the way to the mid-40's. That "strong institutional support" appeared to melt away in a panic.

Avon finally showed a 13 per cent earnings decline in the first quarter of 1974—the first dip in more than a decade. This was followed by another down quarter, and by the summer of 1974 Avon was selling at $30 a share.

Probably the all-time world's-champion super growth stock is IBM. Its record of growth goes back to prehistoric times, and there have been all kinds of mouth-watering stories about people who invested a few thousand dollars in

IBM and became millionaires. There's one about a Miss America–contest winner who put her $75,000 earnings into IBM stock in the mid-50's and by the fall of 1973, between stock splits, dividends and appreciation, had a fortune of $2 million.

A look at IBM's annual report makes it easy to understand why the computer giant has made millions for investors and is such a favorite with the professional money managers.

In the ten years covered by the 1973 annual report, the company has shown a steady pattern of sales and earnings gains that is guaranteed to make any portfolio manager's face light up in the dark (based on recent performance by the professionals, one must assume they work in the dark). In 1964, IBM's sales were $3.2 billion and profits were $467 million, or $3.52 a share. Ten years and five stock dividends later, sales had grown to $11 billion and profits to $1.5 billion, or $10.79 a share.

Because of its magnificent growth record, IBM carries a considerably higher multiple than the run-of-the-list stock. The market looks at past growth and projects it into the future, and that's what the investor is paying for. A dull number like AT&T, which has had its growth pattern marred by an occasional flat year (in 1970 earnings dipped to $2.189 billion from $2.198 billion), has carried a multiple of between 10 and 20, while IBM generally sells at better than 30 times earnings. (The 1974 bear market pushed IBM's multiple down below 15.)

But even IBM's past record is no assurance that earnings will continue to grow at the same price. Furthermore, IBM has been having its problems in court with an assortment of antitrust suits, and since more than half of its earnings come from overseas, the company is vulnerable to troubles abroad.

The 1973 annual report points out that the Justice Department is charging IBM with monopolizing the computer business and wants to break it up. In a private antitrust suit

Telex, a manufacturer of peripheral equipment for computers, had already been granted a $295.5 million judgment (which IBM was appealing), and there were five other suits against IBM seeking total damages of nearly $3.8 billion. All this litigation had its impact on IBM stock, and during 1973, IBM went from a high of 340 to a low of 225.

While the huge claims in the lawsuits would appear to be a real threat to IBM's total worth of $8.8 billion, the IBM financial report indicates that the company was not overly concerned, that it denied the charges and had not set up any contingency reserve to cover damages that may be awarded.

IBM's $8.8 billion net worth (as of December 31, 1973) brings up a point about the effect the price the market puts on growth has had on accounting values and market values.

Price Waterhouse & Company, one of the nation's largest and best-known accounting firms, says that on December 31, IBM was worth $8,812,023,733 and backs that figure with a certification that says the evaluation was confirmed through the application of "generally accepted accounting principles."

The stock market ignores generally accepted accounting principles and will price a growth company like IBM at many times the value the accountants put on it. Even at 225 a share, the lowest price the market had on IBM during that year, the market was saying IBM was worth $32.8 billion (225 times the 146 million shares outstanding). On the other hand, a cyclical company, one with earnings that go up and down with the flow of the economy, might be priced by the market at half its book value or even less.

VIII

READING THE MARKET

THE HIGHER THE ALPHA THE BETA

The gaping disparity between accounting values and market values points up the difficulty in determining even current worth. Future value is infinitely more difficult to figure, but that hasn't stopped an entire industry from trying.

For tax purposes, the U.S. Treasury defines fair market value as "the price at which the property would change hands between a willing buyer and a willing seller when the former is not under any compulsion to buy and the latter is not under any obligation to sell, both parties having reasonable knowledge of the relevant facts."

But if we strike the word "fair" and want to determine "market value" as it refers to the stock market, it comes down to the price at which securities will change hands between a buyer and seller. There is no need for knowledge of relevant facts, and there may well be compulsion for the seller to sell—a margin call or the need for quick cash. The market price deflects the accumulated wisdom, ignorance, fear, hope, greed and many other emotional factors of millions of buyers and sellers.

Wall Street chartists hope to measure all these psychological factors with a dizzying array of heads and shoulders and tops and bottoms and trend lines, while mathematical methodologists seek after the truth with alphas, betas and gammas.

The use of charts predated the coming of the institutional revolution, and I'm sure prehistoric man must have scratched out trend lines with sharp stones on the wall of his cave to predict phases of the moon (it works on phases of the moon). But the beta coefficient can be blamed only on the new breed of sophisticated money managers.

The beta concept is a bit abstruse, but after some hairy discussions with some hairy Ph.D.'s, I think I've got it and hereby pass it on:

Beta is a measure of the volatility of a particular stock or portfolio. It should determine how much a portfolio will rise or fall in relation to movements in the market. The market—as measured by one index or another—is given a beta of 1. The portfolio is given a beta rating based on historical information as to how the stocks in the portfolio moved in relation to the market. If the portfolio tended to have wider swings than the market—that is, moved up more than a rising market and moved down farther than a falling market—the beta would be greater than 1. For instance, a portfolio whose swings were double the market swings would have a beta of 2, while one whose movements were only half as wide as the market's would have a beta of .50.

So a portfolio with a high beta is riskier and would be subject to sharper rises and dips than one with a low beta. All nicely reasoned out if the basic assumption is valid that stocks follow a fixed path relative to the market.

If the theoreticians were content to use beta ratings merely as a guide to the riskiness of a portfolio—to warn the investor that if he buys into a high-beta portfolio he might expect to make lots of money in an up market but could get killed in a down market—I would have no quarrel with them.

But this was not the case. Since beta was such a smash on Wall Street, why not do a little something with alpha? Now we have an alpha rating that's supposed to measure how much better or worse a particular portfolio does than is implied in its beta rating. This is the real test of a money manager, say the alpha people. When a portfolio with a high beta rating can stay alive in a down market while the rest of the high-beta men are falling out of bed, that's good money management.

One institutional investment house that keeps its computer busy tracking mutual funds and has gone in heavily for this alpha-beta nonsense provides a ranking of the funds by alpha rating. For the ten-year period to January 31, 1974, the best job of beating its beta was turned in by a little fund that invests in over-the-counter securities appropriately named the Over-the-Counter Securities Fund. The fund was assigned a beta rating of .49, which indicates it should be about half as volatile as the Standard & Poor's 500 average, yet while the S&P rose 64.59 per cent during the ten-year period, OTC Securities rose 172.64 per cent. This is supposed to imply superior money management—minimizing risk and maximizing return. I think the whole alpha business is a form of mathematical masturbation and the computers could be put to better use counting the bubbles in a bottle of Seven-Up.

It doesn't take a genius to figure out that all alpha is saying is that beta doesn't work and the higher the alpha rating, the larger the error in the beta calculation.

If alpha and beta aren't enough for the Greek-letter enthusiast, there's also a gamma factor kicked around in money-manager circles. This has something to do with how many years' growth has been ground into the current price of a particular growth stock. Beyond that I haven't been able to grasp the point of it. But if someone should start talking about the market and you'd like to join in the conversation without revealing your ignorance of the subject, just look cool and announce:

"My portfolio has a higher gamma factor than anyone else's in this room and I can prove it."

This is guaranteed to raise your status to that of a money maven and turn the conversation away from the market and hopefully to something more stimulating.

As for the chartists, if the price of a stock moved along a trajectory that could be plotted like the path of a guided missile, I'd try to find out what a breakout point looked like. Unfortunately, stock prices are moved by more complex forces than acceleration, mass, angle of inclination and air pressure. Stock prices are moved by people, and people act in strange and mysterious ways—especially professional money managers.

About the only validity the charts have is that there are enough investors who follow them to provide a form of self-fulfilling prophecy. If the charts say buy, the believers buy and drive the price up. But if earnings should fall shortly thereafter, an upside breakout is followed by a severe downside adjustment and a lot of crumpled graph paper.

One chartist whose stuff goes to professional money managers—if I found my banker reading this kind of stuff I'd have him burned at the stake as a witch—had this chart of Simplicity Pattern with the happy news that the stock's closing price on January 30 was an "almost perfect 'cut in half'"—presumably the mid-point between the high and low of the stock. This was supposed to indicate that the "downside risk" was just about nil. A week later there was this announcement referred to in the preceding chapter about Simplicity's lower earnings and there was another almost perfect cut in half. The stock had dropped to 15.

The chartists have developed a literature that makes accountants' footnotes and lawyers' briefs sound like the first chapter of *See Mary Run*. And the amount of statistical trivia is awesome. Some track the hourly changes in the Dow Jones Industrial Averages. One technical service announced that a study of the chart patterns of the Dow Jones Average going back to 1897 showed that an "identifiable" year-end rally had taken place in every year since then. There's statistical information on every squiggle the market has ever taken.

One would expect that grown men could find something more interesting to read than 77 years' worth of graphs.

And listen to this explanation of a particular breed of "resistance line":

Resistance line measurement . . . is based upon two principal determinants of crowd psychology in the market place—price change itself and elapsed time to achieve it. The resistance-line concept attempts to measure these two elements of mass psychology, mathematically weighing both the vertical price-change and the horizontal elapse of time. Resistance lines can be based upon any set of important tops and bottoms. The theory is that a trendline rising at one-third (or two-thirds) the rate of an advance movement is likely to provide resistance to a subsequent decline but if violated, the decline will accelerate at the point of penetration. Similarly, a trendline declining at one third (or two thirds) the rate of a decline movement may provide resistance to a subsequent advance movement, but if penetrated, the advance will accelerate at that point. . . .

The chartist goes on in the only clear sentence in his presentation to say "Sometimes it works, sometimes it does not. . . ." but it's better than garden-variety trend lines.

Some chart books have a disclaimer in fine print, pointing out that technical analysis has its limitations and should not be taken too seriously.

If I had my way, every technical analyst would have to stamp in three-inch letters across every piece of literature he sends out the following caveat:

"This is all bullshit, but it's a living."

IX

MUTUAL FUNDS

THE HIGH COST OF LOSING MONEY

The most common mistake investors make about mutual funds is buying them.

At least, that's what recent performance figures for the average mutual fund clearly indicate. During the five years from 1969 through 1973, the average mutual fund lost 16.33 per cent, meaning that a dollar put into the average mutual fund in 1968 would have dwindled five years later to around 84 cents after adding in dividends received during the period and any capital-gains distributions. If the fund you bought was a load fund and there was a sales charge, knock off another 8 cents, leaving you with 76 cents out of every dollar you invested. And if you really want to get mad at the mutual-fund managers, take a look at what the dollar would buy at the end of 1968 and what it was worth at the end of 1973.

There is a nagging doubt in my mind whether professional money management has any more validity than palmistry, phrenology or astrology. As a matter of fact, I know of one securities analyst whose greatest market coup came from his palmist. It seems this dark lady saw a D in his future. So the analyst went back to his stock lists and came up with Deere, a farm-equipment manufacturer that rode the agricultural boom from 36 to 66, and he became a hero. Of course, he might just as easily have chosen Daylin, a retailer that went from 18 to 5, and he'd have been forced to change palmists.

Over the five years through 1973, the average mutual-fund manager not only lost money for investors, but lost more than he would have had he just ignored his in-depth research reports and bought the popular averages.

While the average fund was losing 16.33 per cent, the Standard & Poor's Index of 425 stocks was down only 3.21 per cent, the S&P 500-stock index was off 6.08 per cent, the Dow Jones Industrial Average was off by 9.84 per cent and the Composite Index of all common stocks on the New York Stock Exchange had dropped 12.02 per cent. In other words, each of these mindless indices had outperformed the cream of the nation's professional money managers during that period.

These performance figures were compiled by the Lipper Analytical Division of Cohn, Delaire & Kaufman, a New York brokerage firm. In the interest of fairness to the mutual-fund managers, I must point out that the Lipper figures for the seven-year period to December 31, 1973, show that the funds' superperformance in 1967–68 was not completely dissipated in the following five years. For the seven years, the average mutual fund was still ahead 33.65 per cent, while the best of the four averages, the S&P 425, was up 28.33 per cent and the worst, the Dow Jones Industrials, showed a gain of only 8.30 per cent.

Also in the interest of fairness, it should be noted that the Lipper comparison of fund performance with the indices is biased in favor of the funds. Calculations for fund performance are adjusted for reinvestment of dividends. The change in an index is measured simply by comparing its level at the beginning of the period with its level at the end. This can make a substantial difference. In 1973, for instance, the S&P 500 was down 17.37 unadjusted, but only 14.71 per cent if dividends were included.

It's been so difficult for the funds merely to outperform the unmanaged averages that American Express Asset Management Company decided early in 1974 to set up a fund to buy 100 shares in every stock making up the Standard & Poor's 500. The fund was to be aimed at institutional investors seeking a reliable, if limited, annual return on their money. Figures for the ten years to the end of 1972 put the S&P among the top 11 per cent of mutual funds and pension-fund managers on the basis of return on investment.

Perhaps large institutions would be satisfied with money management that keeps up with the averages, but the individual investor apparently is not. Individual investors have been backing away from mutual funds, cashing in their shares and looking for someplace to hide. In 1972 and 1973, mutual-fund holders redeemed $12.3 billion worth of shares. New sales could not keep up, and the result was a net withdrawal of $3 billion. Redemptions continued to outrun sales until the spring of 1974, when the money-market funds began to attract enough new cash to put the industry back into a net-sales position. Nevertheless, in July of 1974 total net assets of mutual-fund companies were down to $37.7 billion from $50.9 billion just one year earlier.

A good part of the funds' troubles can be traced to their own efforts to oversell performance. In the happy days of the 1967–68 bull market, funds were turning up with increases of 100 per cent a year or better, and the public poured in billions of dollars.

In 1969 the market turned around, there were several scandals involving the use of lettered stock (stock that was carried at a market value that did not exist, since sale of the stock was restricted) and there was a tendency for the funds to keep their own portfolio issues hot by bidding up the prices themselves. A fund with a large block of, say, Four Seasons Nursing Homes could keep upward pressure on the price through additional purchases. The money was pouring in, and it was no problem getting new money to keep a prop under old mistakes.

But when the market turned, the new money stopped flowing and the old money started running out and the mutual-fund salesmen left the business for something with a little more stability. All this happening at once left the industry in a state of disarray, but in 1974 there was still $40 billion or thereabouts in the industry and it was doing its best to regroup and establish a place among the various options we have for saving and possibly making money.

The industry has a mind-blowing variety of funds—load and no-load, closed-end and open-end, dual-purpose, growth, income, balanced, bond, leveraged, hedge funds, even funds that invest in other funds. The latest entry in this financial laundry list is the money-market fund—an investment vehicle designed originally to provide a temporary haven for idle funds. However, as inflation drove short-term interest rates to unheard-of peaks, the money-market fund became the top seller in the fund industry's product line.

To begin winding through the fund maze, let's start with load and no-load funds. Load funds are sold to the public through brokers or dealers or special sales agencies, and the investor pays a sales charge of about 8 per cent on shares he buys. No-load shares are sold by the funds themselves, and there is no sales charge.

In my opinion, there is absolutely no good reason for an investor with a modicum of intelligence to pay a sales charge to buy stock in a mutual fund.

Over the years I have conscientiously but vainly sought a sensible reason for the sales charge—I mean sensible from the investor's viewpoint.

The most popular rationalization is an old chestnut in the business about how mutual funds are sold and not bought and without salesmen nobody would buy them.

That may sound eminently reasonable to the sponsors of a mutual fund, but it doesn't earn the investor one nickel. It's tough enough to make money in the stock market without starting out by giving the market an extra 8 per cent edge.

Another tack taken to justify the sales load to the investor was that load funds, with their salesmen out constantly bringing in new money, were able to perform better. The flow of new money allowed the load funds to take advantage of opportunities that might otherwise have eluded them. My own feeling is that the pressure of new money coming in is just as likely to encourage bad investments as good ones.

I have also been told that load is really insignificant in the great scheme of things and that performance is all the investor should concern himself with. If you pay an 8 per cent sales charge and the fund goes up 20 per cent, you're much better off than if you buy a no-load fund that goes down 20 per cent. Right. Except that there's no correlation between load, no-load and performance. This should not come as any surprise, but if you need figures to back up something that is obvious on the face of it, a study of 358 load funds and 106 no-loads by Fundscope, a Los Angeles–based magazine and statistical service, found that there was no significant difference in the performance of load and no-load funds.

What about service? A salesman can advise the investor and help him choose the plan that best fits his particular situation. That may be true, but there are also salesmen who will fit the investor's program to the salesman's own particular needs and the only service the investor will get is the kind a bull gives to a cow. On balance, the service rendered doesn't merit the price exacted.

Before leaving the matter of load vs. no-load funds, just one more argument should be knocked down. In my search

for economic justification of sales loads, I have been told
that sales charges are built into just about everything we
buy, so why make this big thing about mutual funds? What
about insurance, for instance? The portion of premiums that
goes for salesmen's commissions is much higher than the
mutual-fund load. That may be true, and if you find a no-
load insurance company, use it.

If no-loads make no sales charge, how do they make
money?

To explain this, it's necessary to go into the basic structure
of a mutual fund. The fund is set up by a sponsor, who must
round up $100,000 to get it started. The sponsor will set up a
management company—a separate entity from the fund itself—and the management company enters into an agreement with the fund to handle the investments. This contract
sets up the fee that the fund will pay the management company—generally in the neighborhood of ½ of 1 per cent of
the net assets of the fund. If the fund is to be a load vehicle,
the sponsor might also organize a sales agency to sell the
shares. After the whole package is scrutinized by the Securities and Exchange Commission and approved (the prospec-
tus says specifically that the issue has not been approved or
disapproved by the SEC, but that's a bureaucratic copout;
just try to sell shares in a mutual fund without SEC approval
and see how fast they'll put you away), shares may then
be sold.

Anyhow, the mutual fund itself is just that—with profits
and losses shared by stockholders. The sponsor of a no-load
fund makes his money from the management fee. The sponsor of a load fund gets his from the management fee and a
share of the sales charge. Also, many funds, load and no-load,
are sponsored by brokerage firms, which can channel commissions on fund transactions through the sponsoring broker.
This is an obvious conflict of interest, and the practice has
been subject to much criticism.

When a brokerage firm manages a mutual fund, there is the ever-present temptation to churn the fund's portfolio in order to generate commission business for the broker. This temptation increases as noncaptive brokerage business declines, and over the past few years the brokerage industry has gone through some pretty trying times.

In defense, the brokers concede the temptation but contend there has been little evidence to show that brokers have been corrupted by it. Furthermore, since management fees are based on the size of the funds and funds must show performance to attract investors, churning for the sake of commissions would be self-defeating.

The basic difference between closed-end and open-end funds is found in the method of selling shares.

An open-end fund will issue new shares as the demand requires and pay out cash to shareholders who want to redeem their shares at net asset value (the market value of the fund's portfolio divided by the number of fund shares outstanding). A closed-end fund has a fixed number of shares outstanding, and these are traded in the open market. If you want to buy shares in Madison Fund, a large closed-end fund, you buy them on the New York Stock Exchange through your broker, just as you would buy shares in American Telephone or IBM, and pay the standard commission. The fund never sees your money, and the price you pay, while related to net asset value, varies with market psychology. Some closed-end funds sell at a discount from asset value, others at a premium.

In pricing closed-end fund shares, there are two levels of insanity at work. First there are the original market factors that price the stock in the fund's portfolio. These give it the net asset value. Then there are the factors that go into pricing the stock of the closed-end fund which take into consideration the management of the fund. If the market believes the management is superior, the fund will sell at a premium.

If the market thinks the fund's management in the future will underperform the market, then the stock will sell at a discount.

The effect of this aberration is that it is possible to buy $15 worth of marketable securities for $10 if the closed-end fund is selling at a discount, or you can pay $20 for the same $15 worth of securities if the stock is selling at a premium. As a rule, when the stock market is in a bull phase most closed-end funds sell at a premium, and when there's gloom on Wall Street the closed-end funds will sell at a discount.

The relative merits of closed-end funds as opposed to open-end funds are difficult to fathom. In the past few years, when redemptions of open-end shares were high and sales of new shares lagged, the closed-end management companies had an advantage. In making investment decisions they didn't have to keep looking back over their shoulder to be sure they had enough cash in the till to cover redemptions. They could concentrate on losing money in the market.

On a weekend in February of 1974, during the energy-crisis-inspired bear market, a listing in *Barron's* of 13 diversified closed-end common stock funds showed all but two selling at a discount from net asset value. Madison Fund, for example, with a net asset value of $13.03, was selling at 9¾—a 25.2 per cent discount.

Among a group of specialized closed-end funds, only three carried premiums. The market gave the largest to ASA, an investment company with its money in South African gold mines, which was selling at 35.8 per cent above net asset value.

Dual-purpose funds also provide an opportunity to pick up "bargains" in terms of market value. The duals are closed-end funds set up to provide income for those interested in current return and capital gains for those interested in appreciation. The concept is delicious and came into vogue in 1967 when the market was flying. The duals have two classes of stock, generally representing half the capitalization of the fund. Income shares get the dividends from the whole portfolio but do not participate in capital appreciation. The capital shares get all the appreciation and depreciation but forgo current income. The income shares must be redeemed at their original offering price after a fixed period of time, and if there's any deficiency, this comes out of the hides of the capital-share owners.

There are nine major dual-purpose funds operating, and maturity dates range from 1979 for American Dual Vest to 1985 for Hemisphere Fund.

In a rising market, the capital shares gain the benefits that would ordinarily have accrued to the income shares, but in a falling market, the capital shares must assume their own losses plus the losses that would have been taken by the income shares.

As in the case of other closed-end funds, the market price of a dual fund will reflect the prices of the underlying securities and an additional market factor that translates into a discount or premium. Early in 1974, both the capital and the income shares of most dual funds were being sharply discounted in the market.

The income shares in the dual funds provide the same type of capital-gains possibilities as discount bonds. Typically, at one point in February of 1974, American Dual Vest income shares were selling at a market price of 11⅞ and yielding 7.1 per cent at that price. These shares mature in 1979, when they will be redeemed at $15. On that same date American Dual Vest had capital shares worth $6.57 each as additional coverage for the payment of the income shares at maturity. These capital shares, incidentally, were selling at 5⅝, for a discount of 14.4 per cent.

Generally, funds are classified by objective. Growth funds look for capital appreciation; growth-and-income funds try for some capital appreciation and current income; balanced funds strike a balance between stocks and bonds and so on. But objectives are not always matched by results. Growth funds did very well during the go-go days, but since then many have been shrink funds. The growth funds are more volatile and admittedly take greater risks in the hope of greater rewards.

The growth-and-income funds and the balanced funds outperformed the growth funds in recent years because they stayed away from the high-flying volatile sector of the market and because yield on bonds has been relatively high. One unusual fund that capitalized on the high yield in bonds combined with the safety of Federal Government issues was the Fund for U.S. Government Securities, which from a standing start in October of 1969 ran its assets up to around $100 million by the end of 1973 and showed an increase in net asset value of 35 per cent for the period.

This fund deals in "riskless" securities of the Federal Government and agencies of the Federal Government, and its performance depends on how well it can choose between long-term and short-term securities. If it gets locked into long-term Government bonds and long-term interest rates rise, the "riskless" securities can sink sharply in value.

There are also hedge funds, which are permitted to sell short and thus make money in down markets, but they have not performed well. Leveraged funds, which use borrowed money in their investment activities, have also proved disappointing.

Mutual funds are great trend followers, and during the 1967–68 performance era sponsors were looking for gimmicks that would permit them to keep more of the money they were making for the ungrateful stockholders. Compensation plans were worked out that would reward superior performance and penalize the laggards. Most of these plans were keyed to performance in relation to one of the popular averages.

One of my favorite funds of that era was an outfit called Competitive Capital Fund, set up in March of 1968. Not only did it provide special compensation for beating the Dow Jones Industrial Average; it also had five different money managers competing against one another on performance. As the fund progressed, the manager who performed best would get the largest portion of new money coming in and a chance for increased compensation. The theory here was that investment funds would flow to the superior managers and the managers who fell behind would be fired. This would be the ultimate in sophisticated money management and nobody could lose. The fund had to be a fantastic success.

The management-fee schedule provided a minimum of ⅜ of 1 per cent of net assets a year if performance was poor and up to ⅞ of 1 per cent of assets if the fund doubled the Dow—increased at twice the rate of increase of the Dow Jones Industrial Average.

In its first nine months of operation, Competitive Capital did pretty well. Its assets grew to about $100 million and it was up 21 per cent, compared with an increase of just over 4 per cent for the Dow in 1968. The concept was working, and it was full speed ahead.

The next year it fell on its ass.

Competitive Capital dropped 26 per cent and was ranked number 335 among a list of 378 funds tracked by the Lipper organization that year. By the end of 1973, Competitive Capital was down to $27 million in assets and had shown five-year growth of minus 57 per cent. A dollar invested in Competitive Capital at the beginning of 1969 had dwindled to 43 cents.

If you plan to invest in a mutual fund, you should look up the fund's track record before you put your money in. This is sound advice, and like feeding chicken soup to a corpse, it won't hurt. But it won't help.

In 1968, the top-performing fund was Mates Investment Fund, a growth vehicle that shot ahead 153 per cent until it was suspended on December 20, 1968, because of hanky-panky involving lettered stock and other irregularities disturbing to the Securities and Exchange Commission. A Mates share was worth $15.51 just prior to its suspension. By the end of the next year, Mates had fallen to $5.71 a share.

It continued to do badly, and by the end of 1973 its assets had dropped from $23.8 million to about $2 million and the value of each Mates share had fallen 78 per cent over those five years. Fred Mates, the head of the fund, was rediscovered in 1974, running a singles bar on New York's upper East Side.

The number two fund in the great go-go year of 1968 was the Neuwirth Fund, a swinging growth-and-income fund that came up with a 90 per cent increase. The next year, this same super growth vehicle dropped 17.45 per cent and was number 263 in the Lipper ratings. For the five-year period to the end of 1973, Neuwirth dropped 43.46 per cent and ranked 293 in performance. (For the seven years covering 1967 through 1973, Neuwirth could still boast a 330.55 per cent increase because of a wild jump in 1967 and the 90 per cent rise in 1968.)

In 1968, the highly touted Manhattan Fund, managed by the legendary Gerry Tsai, finished dead last—number 310 out of 310 funds followed by the Lipper service. It remained a dud through the next five years and saw its assets shrink from $450 million to $100 million and its per-share value drop 57.52 per cent.

Far and away the best-performing fund in the five years to the end of 1973 was a growth-and-income fund called International Investors. The company started out to invest in foreign securities but evolved into a South African gold-mining-share fund.

The price of gold started moving upward in 1968 after the

United States and other industrial nations abandoned efforts to keep the price of gold at $35 an ounce and set up the two-tier gold market. As the price of gold started moving up, gold-mining stocks did likewise. The big move in the gold price came in 1972 and 1973 amid a series of international monetary crises, and International Investors was perfectly postured. It gained 58.35 per cent in 1972, ranking second in the Lipper standings, and in 1973 it gained 94.43 per cent and came in first. For the five years beginning in 1969 International Investors also ranked number one, with a 170.23 per cent gain. Its performance, as is to be expected, attracted great gobs of new money, and assets ballooned from $4 million in 1971 to $67 million at the end of 1973.

Whether International Investors keeps growing depends on what happens to the price of gold. Nobody can predict with any certainty that gold will continue to climb, so the past record of success is of little significance in choosing today's investment. I don't believe there are superior money managers. There are lucky money managers and unlucky money managers, and there's no way of knowing when the dice will turn cold in the hands of a Gerry Tsai or in the hands of five managers of Competitive Capital.

With the erratic performance turned in by the mutual-fund managers as a class and by bank trust departments (which will be explored in the next chapter), it's difficult to concede the existence of money management. At this point, I'm not convinced that it exists and I'm not convinced that it doesn't exist. I am convinced that given the present state of the art, money management is not worth paying a hell of a lot for, and the direction the mutual-fund industry might take is to show it can handle (not manage) your investments cheaply and efficiently, and that economies of scale in handling pools of money make it worthwhile for the investor to turn over his investable funds to an organization that knows its way around Wall Street. In return for this service, the investor should be willing to pay a small handling charge.

There is one favorable aspect of mutual-fund investment which is unassailable, and that's its value as a form of forced savings. Friends who have invested in funds and have been disappointed in their performance nevertheless concede that if they hadn't put the money into mutual funds, they would have spent it on foolishness. At least they managed to salvage something.

X

BANK TRUST
DEPARTMENTS

WHERE DID WRIGHT PATMAN GO WRONG?

At one time, life in the trust department of a bank was simple and secure. The trust manager bought some Jersey Standard (now Exxon), some American Telephone & Telegraph, maybe a couple more blue-chip common stocks and a bunch of 4 per cent bonds, and the rest was just bookkeeping, coupon clipping and holding the hands of rich widows to explain that banks weren't supposed to make a lot of money on trust accounts; they were there to preserve capital and earn a reasonable income—4 per cent conservative, or maybe 6 per cent if you want to speculate.

Then came the era of performance, and the banks were sucked in with the rest of the investment world. If mutual funds could double your money in a year, why the hell don't the banks get off their butts? Interest rates took off, adding more pressure for performance. In 1970 top-grade long-term bonds went over 9 per cent, wiping out billions in values of older, lower-yielding bonds and sharply raising the sights of what investors expected as a return on their money. Inflation came along to further complicate the formerly peaceful lives of the bank money managers. The old 6 per cent yield would never make it in this environment. So the banks went after action, and they got it. They went after "growth" stocks.

Banks traditionally have been secretive about the operations of their trust departments, contending that they have a confidential relationship with clients and it's nobody's business but the client's if the bank is performing well or poorly. But that's all changing now, and little by little the banks are opening up the windows and letting the fresh air in. At this writing there is also legislative movement toward directing banks to make the same kind of disclosure of their trust-department operations as the mutual funds are required to do. The funds report quarterly on their purchases, sales and current investment positions.

Part of the pressure on the banks for disclosure stems from their concentration of investment in what had come to be known as the Nifty Fifty. Stocks such as IBM, Xerox, Avon Products, Eastman Kodak, American Home Products and Simplicity Pattern were in great demand among all institutional buyers, and the result was a great disparity in the price/earnings ratios of the favored fifty and the rest of the market. This became the two-tier market—the upper tier being the favored fifty and the lower tier, everything else.

There was a great cry that the banks' concentration on this limited number of stocks was destroying the rest of the market. Companies not included in the fifty had no way of raising capital, the over-the-counter market was going down the pipe and the prices of the favorites were dangerously high. There was an organization formed made up of listed companies that were beyond the pale. This group pushed for full disclosure of bank trust-department operations and even sought to limit how much stock an institution could buy in a company and regulate the selling practices of institutions so they could not dump huge blocks in one day and instantly destroy the price of a particular issue.

The banks never accepted the assumption that they concentrated investments in the small group of vestal virgins, but everyone else did, and a look at the holdings of several bank trust departments certainly gave one the feeling of *déjà vu*.

The favored fifty earned the loyalty of the banks for several reasons, chief of which was the record of uninterrupted profit growth.

The first-tier stocks also met the requirement of large capitalization, since banks, with their huge flow of funds, can't fool around with small companies. The favored fifty served the bank trust departments well until 1973, when the real world intruded. A few were destroyed by the flat-quarter syndrome (Avon, Simplicity). Sturdy old reliable IBM, which managed to maintain its growth pattern, was rocked by a series of unfavorable court rulings and the stock price went into a skid. Other firms were hurt by the energy shortage. Disney Productions, superstar, was shattered by the energy crisis, since such attractions as Disneyland in California and Disney World in Florida were dependent on the free and growing use of that energy gobbler, the automobile. McDonald's Corporation, another institutional favorite, was also battered by the gas shortage.

Disney was hit with a flat quarter at the beginning of 1973 (18 cents against 19 cents) and then took another clobbering from the energy crisis. After reaching a high of 123⅞ early in 1973, it plunged to 70 by mid-year and was in the high 30's in the summer of 1974. McDonald's ran up to 77 in 1973 but by mid-1974 had dropped into the 40's.

The collapse of the two-tier market carried through 1973 and into 1974 as the market, shaken by the fall of some highly visible one-decision superstocks, went through an agonizing re-evaluation of multiples. In the process, the bank trust departments took a beating. A one-decision stock, by the way, is the portfolio manager's favorite illusion. It's a stock you buy and forget about. You never have to make a decision on when to sell, because earnings go up indefinitely in a pre-determined pattern and the market price continues to appreciate. A two-decision stock is a pain. You have to keep watching it, trying to figure out whether it's gone as high as it is going to go, or whether a sudden price weakness is a market aberration or a basic downtrend. It's just too much trouble, and besides, when you have to make two decisions, you can make two mistakes. If you make one decision, you can just make one mistake. Since bank portfolio managers are very good at arithmetic, it's logical that they will choose the one-decision stock.

As I mentioned, the banks have recently begun to open up on their trust-department operations, and their timing could not have been worse.

Private pensions as a group took a shocking loss. The Securities and Exchange Commission reported that in 1973 private pension funds added about $4.6 billion to common stock holdings, yet at year end total holdings had declined from $113.4 billion to $88 billion—a loss of $25.4 billion. Add to this the new money invested and we have a $30 billion blood bath suffered by pension-fund beneficiaries. Most of this loss was presided over by the money managers at the nation's bank trust departments.

In 1973, the best performer of the major New York banks in handling common-stock investments of pension funds was the Bank of New York. It lost only 11.2 per cent.

What's so great about losing 11.2 per cent?

Well Morgan Guaranty, the biggest in the trust field, lost 20.78 per cent, and Bankers Trust Company, another giant, dropped 28.4 per cent. These figures reflect the fall of the two-tier market.

Data on the 1973 performance of a number of major bank trust departments were first disclosed in Robert Metz's column in *The New York Times*. Mr. Metz, obviously deluged with complaints from bankers, ran a follow-up showing three years' results, giving the banks a chance to prove that 1973 was a fluke and in prior years they had done much better. Again, the Bank of New York, with $4.6 billion under management, came up with the best record of the New York majors—a compound annual return for the three years (1971 through 1973) of 8.3 per cent. However, Morgan Guaranty's three-year record was a meager 5.6 per cent, and Bankers Trust showed a compound growth of only 2.6 per cent a year for the three years. That growth figure includes appreciation as well as dividend income.

The pension-fund accounts do not cover the complete operations of trust departments, which also handle personal trusts and investment-advisory accounts. However, it's fairly safe to assume that the pension-fund performance is typical of the results as a whole.

In fact, this might be a bit generous, since most banks also have special equity accounts—smaller and much more aggressive pools of other peoples' money. The 1973 results in those accounts were downright obscene and would tend to pull the over-all results even lower. In 1973, United States Trust Company, one of the big five in the trust business, had a plunge of 42 per cent in its special equity fund.

The average 1973 decline of 12 of these aggressive equity funds was 31 per cent, while the average of 42 of the large bank pension trust funds was down 19.2 per cent, according to Charles J. Elia of *The Wall Street Journal*, another of my favorite financial columnists.

As of December 31, 1972, Morgan Guaranty had under management the largest single pool of investment funds anywhere—$27.4 billion. At the end of 1973, the pool had dropped to $23.6 billion. Morgan reportedly received nearly $1 billion in new money that year, so it can be assumed that the total loss was in the vicinity of $5 billion ($5,000,000,-000). Wow! Who said the Big Guys make all the money on Wall Street and the Little Guys get murdered?

On the basis of 5.2 million shares of IBM held by Morgan

Guaranty at the end of 1972, the price change in that stock alone would have meant a loss of about a half-billion dollars.

Within a bank's trust department there are some trusts handled on an individual basis and others which hold shares in common or commingled funds. The common funds are for personal trust accounts and commingled funds for the pension accounts, which are tax-exempt. This in effect sets up bank-operated mutual funds in which the individual trusts own shares. At Morgan Guaranty, about $4 billion of its trust funds were in these types of accounts at the end of 1972, and the largest of these commingled accounts was its SSI (Special Situation Investments) Equities Fund, which had $971 million invested in common stocks of relatively small companies.

The over-all criteria Morgan Guaranty set for this fund as outlined in a report issued by the bank in May of 1973 are as follows:

•Companies of known managerial strength and integrity, identifiable by checking with reliable sources;
•Product line or managerial concept with a high degree of uniqueness and competitive advantage;
•Above-average return on total capital and common equity, or marked improvement occurring in these returns if they are not already above average;
•Realistic possibility that earnings per share will increase at a compounded annual rate of 15 per cent or more;
•Realistic possibility that price will double in not more than five years.

Morgan Guaranty goes on to state that individual trusts are limited in the percentage of their total funds that can be invested in the SSI Equities Fund and that as of the end of 1972, participating trusts had about 8.9 per cent of their common-stock portfolios in SSI units.

In 1973, SSI Equities Fund slumped 39.46 per cent.

So how "realistic" is the possibility that a company's earnings will grow at 15 per cent a year compounded and its stock will double in price in five years or less?

And despite the bombing that the so-called growth stocks took in 1973, the banks have not given up the concept. Early the following year, the head of the United States Trust Company's investment operation told Mr. Elia of *The Wall Street Journal*, "We believe based on our economic thinking that quality growth stocks are still the best place to put your money for the long term."

The dream of never-ending growth dies hard.

The nation's number one critic of banks and bank trust departments is Wright Patman, Chairman of the House Banking and Currency Committee. Congressman Patman has spent nearly fifty years in the House of Representatives and has built a career sniping at banks. Let the banks raise the prime interest rate and you can be sure there will be a statement out of Washington from Patman's office condemning the unconscionable profiteering of bankers.

In July of 1968, Congressman Patman released a voluminous report entitled Commercial Banks and Their Trust Activities: Emerging Influence on the American Economy. The report focused on the huge stockholdings of bank trust departments and the number of major corporations in which the banks, through their trust divisions, held large blocks of stock. The report also expressed concern over bankers' serving on boards of industrial corporations and the fact that one-quarter of all bank trust assets was concentrated in just five banks—Morgan Guaranty, Bankers Trust Company, Chase Manhattan Bank, First National City Bank and United States Trust Company.

While all this is certainly legitimate cause for concern, the report spent little time explaining that the trust assets were not assets of the banks but other people's money being managed or mismanaged by the banks.

More recently, two Senate subcommittees issued another

report, this one hitting at banks for using "nominee" registrations for trust-division-held stock. The Senate report indicated that banks used financial pseudonyms to hide their operations.

In a reply published in the February, 1974, issue of *Finance* magazine, Samuel R. Callaway, head of Morgan's trust division, explains rather plausibly that nominee accounts are used to speed up and simplify the transfer of stocks. Furthermore, he says, "A list of nominees and the institutions they represent is readily available from the American Society of Corporate Secretaries."

Mr. Callaway concedes, however, that bank trust departments have been too secretive about their operations.

"For their part," he says,

managers of bank trust departments could help to dispel the aura of mystery that still surrounds trust administration. We could do this by admitting that too often in the past we may have confused silence with discretion, and by moving ahead now to publish—in a format acceptable to all institutional investors—more of the facts and figures about trust activities which do not impair the right of clients and beneficiaries to confidentiality in the trust relationship.

As for me, the question is not whether to disclose or not to disclose or how great an economic power the banks have through their trust departments. To me, the question is, what the hell kind of money management is it that loses 39.46 per cent in one year?

The pension-fund money doesn't belong to the banks. It belongs to the millions of workers and is supposed to provide a measure of security for them. This is not the kind of money that banks should commit in the name of a cockamamie concept of super growth stocks that pay little or nothing in dividends and, in the interest of growth, make unwarranted acquisitions, open stores that shouldn't be open, fool around with their accounting or resort to fraud.

O.K., if bonds are a disaster and growth stocks are an illusion, what's a bank trust department to do?

That's a tough question, and I don't pretend to have the complete answer. But I do think the banks should stop shooting for the big move in stocks and look for an investment strategy that will give them a reasonable return in an inflationary environment. This suggests a movement away from the high-flying growth stocks to the more prosaic numbers that pay real dividends and retain some of their earnings for moderate future growth.

A dividend, current or future, is the only reason anyone, particularly a bank, should pay anything for a stock, but the recent emphasis on capital gains has blurred this truth. If the banks, with their huge buying power, let it be known that stocks that don't pay dividends will be passed over, we could develop a market on a sounder footing than the one that cost bank trust departments all those billions in 1973. Just as the banks' demand for growth forced public corporations to that concept, a philosophy of reasonable current return could turn corporate America to a policy of pay now and grow later.

I'm not knocking growth per se. I'm all in favor of happy corporations increasing profits year after year. The need is for a change in emphasis—from growth at any price to growth tempered by common sense. Surely a company in a new field should be expected to grow and encouraged in that direction, but this is not the ball game for pension-fund money. Let the crapshooters and the long-shot bettors work the supergrowth market.

As for bonds, the bank trust departments could learn from their own lending departments. Although banks make a point of keeping their trust and lending operations at arm's length, I don't think even Congressman Patman would object if the lending officers explained to the trust people that long-term loans at fixed rates are extremely dangerous.

When a bank makes a long-term loan, it generally uses a formula for a floating rate. A typical 10-year bank loan would set the interest rate at ½ point above the prime interest rate, with a floor and possibly a ceiling. Yet over in the trust department, they buy municipal bonds that lock up clients' money for 20 or 30 years at 5 per cent or corporate bonds at 8 per cent, maturing in the twenty-first century.

A fixed-interest long-term bond, given an inflation-prone economic environment, is not a reasonable way to raise money, and the rash of floating-rate bonds that followed Citicorp's $650 million issue in June, 1974, shows that the investment community is finally getting the message.

XI

FINALE

COMMON-SENSE INVESTING

Don't invest in the stock market if you can't afford to lose. There are no guarantees on Wall Street.

Don't buy long-term fixed-interest bonds unless you're prepared to give up part of your principal for the assurance of a fixed return. Ditto for preferred stock.

As I mentioned earlier, floating-rate bonds are sensible, conservative investments that offer a fair return and some protection against inflation. The first major issue of that type in the United States was floated by Citicorp, parent of First National City Bank, in July, 1974, although similar issues had been sold for some time in Europe. Citibank originally planned to sell $250 million worth of the 15-year notes, but the response from the market was so strong that the bank holding company decided to increase the offering to $850 million. However, there was a big fuss over the issue by savings banks and the Federal Reserve Board on the ground that the Citicorp issue would drain too much money out of savings accounts. So Citicorp revised the terms and cut the offering to $650 million. Investors were offered at least 9.7

per cent interest until May 31, 1975. After that, the interest rate would float at 1 per cent above the three-month-Treasury-bill rate until maturity in 1989. In addition, investors were offered the opportunity twice a year to cash in the notes at full face value starting June 1, 1976.

The Citicorp offering was followed by sales of similar notes by the Chase Manhattan Corporation, Mellon National Corporation and others, including one by the New York Bank for Savings, which offered a higher return—10 per cent until May 31, 1975, a floating rate of 1¼ point above the Treasury-bill rate after that date and a floor of 7½ per cent. The New York Bank for Savings issue was shorter-term than the others, maturing in 1981, but it had no provision for redemption prior to maturity.

These notes should not be confused with bank deposits just because the issuers are bank-related. They are debts of the corporations issuing them, and they do not carry the $40,000 in Federal insurance that covers savings-account deposits. But with inflation carrying interest rates to previously unheard-of levels, a floating rate protects the investor against the capital loss suffered by those holding fixed-rate bonds.

Another popular and sensible investment vehicle for an inflationary period is the money-market mutual funds. These, like floating-rate bonds, were spawned by inflation and the high interest rates that accompany inflation.

They invest money in short-term money-market instruments that are regarded as cash equivalents. These include bank certificates of deposit, commercial paper, U.S. securities and banker's acceptances. These are investments which corporations have used for years as a way to keep idle funds working and earning interest. Because these instruments are generally sold only in large denominations ($100,000 for certificates of deposit, for example), the public has not had the chance to become familiar with them. Also, the yield used to be so low that it didn't pay to bother unless big money was involved. But as interest rates rose (CD's were paying over 12 per cent in July, 1974), these money-market funds proliferated and attracted tons of money. One of the first in the business was a New York company called Reserve Fund, which started in 1971 and by mid-1974 was managing over $200 million.

These funds operate by pooling the money of small investors and putting it into the kind of paper previously available only to the Big Boys. Most are no-load vehicles. In addition to the Reserve Fund, the Dreyfus organization has a money-market fund (Dreyfus Liquid Assets), the people who run a fund in Government securities in Pittsburgh have one called Money Market Management, the Fidelity group runs the Fidelity Daily Income Trust in Boston and there are a number of others.

Generally, the money-market funds charge ½ of a percentage point as a management fee and another half-point to cover expenses. This means that if the portfolio is invested in 12 per cent CD's, the yield to the investor would be 11 per cent. The interest is credited on a daily basis and will move up and down as interest rates change. The minimum purchase requirement in some is $1,000 and in others is $5,000. Money invested can usually be withdrawn with just a day's notice.

A few of the mutual-fund organizations have set up money-market funds with sales loads, but I won't even bother to tell you who they are. If there's no justification for a sales load on a mutual fund with a stock or bond portfolio, there's even less in the case of a fund that's supposed to take short-term money. With an 8 per cent load it could take you a year just to break even, and if interest rates decline during that time you're a loser. I know of one fund that charges an 8¾ per cent load; another, 4¼ per cent and a third, 1 per cent. But even 1 per cent is too much.

The money-market funds serve as convenient places to hide during periods of extremely high interest rates. When rates come down, the place to put surplus funds is in the stock market.

For the crapshooters, there's the option market. Options have been sold and bought for years through put and call houses in an informal over-the-counter market. (Puts are options to sell a stock at a specified price during a specified period of time, and calls are options to buy at a particular price within a fixed period.) In April of 1973, the Chicago Board of Trade set up the Chicago Board Options Exchange (CBOE) to trade options in a central market place.

The CBOE offered the trader a chance to take his profit (or loss) on the sale of the option itself rather than having to exercise it. Calls expire at the end of January, April, July and October and start trading about 9 months before their expiration dates. The CBOE started trading calls on 32 New York Stock Exchange issues—ranging alphabetically from AT&T to Xerox—and, while the stock market was having a terrible time with low volume and falling prices, the CBOE was an instant success. It offered the speculator a chance to get in on the action of a blue-chip stock with an investment of just a fraction of the price of the underlying stock. Although most call buyers lost money (at least through July of 1974), the chance to make big money with small investments attracted the long-shot players, and volume boomed.

An article in *Barron's* pointed out that of the 89 options available in the CBOE scheduled to expire in July, 1974, all but 9 were worthless on the last day of trading prior to expiration.

While July was a stock-market horror and not a typical month, it's safe to assume that with the market heading mostly down between April, 1973, and July, 1974, buyers of calls did poorly. The leverage in a call that can mean sharp profits in a climbing market can produce total wipe-out with a relatively small price decline. A $2.50 option on a $40 stock can double in value with a $2.50 increase in the underlying stock price or disappear with a 2½-point decline.

In the year ended June 30, 1974, the value of options traded on the CBOE jumped to $109.4 million from $29.7 million. With this success, the CBOE was pushing to trade options in more issues and also planning to add puts to its product line. Other stock exchanges are getting into the business.

Terry Mayer, national sales manager for Bache & Company, told *The New York Times* in August of 1974 that since the CBOE's inception, a majority of option buyers had lost money while a majority of option writers had made money.

Option writing has the effect of limiting risk in exchange for giving up the chance of big profits in the underlying stock. An owner of 100 shares of stock who agrees to sell a call on that stock gets his premium for the call, around 10 to 15 per cent of the stock price, and he also continues to get the dividends this stock paid until the option is exercised. If the price of the stock goes down, the premium helps to ease the pain of the loss.

If the price goes up, the option writer must give up his stock for the option price. If he wants to hold on to his shares, he can go out and buy a call himself.

The writing of options has come to be a device through which managers of pension funds and other large pools of money can increase the yield on their investments. Since these money managers are concerned principally with the return they can get on their investments and are not shooting for big stock moves, the extra money coming in through the sale of options helps to swell interest and dividend income. When CBOE first started, trust departments of national banks were prohibited from dealing in options in any manner. In July of 1974, however, the Comptroller of the Currency conceded that writing options on shares already held (covered options) was an appropriate investment activity for trust departments, and he lifted the ban.

All in all, options are for sophisticated investors ("sophisticated investor" is a Wall Street euphemism for a customer who generates lots of commissions). Losses can be swift and deadly, but the gains can be sweet. As long as you know what you're doing and can survive the losses without jeopardizing the mortgage payments, enjoy.

The more conservative investors should buy blue-chip stocks that *pay dividends*.

Figure return on your investment as the amount of the dividend plus the portion of earnings plowed back into the business. The payment of a dividend that has some reasonable relationship to the stock price acts as a discipline on the company. It's not so easy to puff up earnings if you're forced to pay out a good part of those earnings in cash to stockholders.

Buy growth stocks if you like, but don't kid yourself. The company will not grow forever, and don't pay too high a price for growth. If a stock is selling at 25 times earnings or more, be careful. In playing for the bigger moves in stocks, set yourself a target on the upside and a bail-out point on the downside. As the stock moves up (assuming it does) you can move the bail-out point higher, but don't fool with your upside target. If the stock hits the price you set for yourself, take your money and run. Greed has done in more stock-market players than all the bear markets in history.

Don't buy on inside information. People on the inside of a company are the worst judges of their own stock values. I've yet to meet a company president who doesn't think Wall Street is undervaluing his company's stock. Only once did I invest on the basis of an insider's telling me about his company's great prospects. It was the one investment I made in a corporation that ultimately wound up in the bankruptcy courts. Furthermore, acting on inside information is illegal, so you're getting a double benefit: you can feel self-righteous about doing the right thing, and the chances are you're saving yourself some money.

Don't buy mutual funds and pay a sales charge. You're getting nothing for your money.

Look at no-load funds as part of a long-term savings program.

Consider buying closed-end funds at a discount. You'll be getting the same kind of portfolio as you would find in any other mutual fund, but you get extra leverage. If the market turns up, the chances are that the closed-end fund will swing to a premium and you can get an extra profit. On the downside, the discount might get bigger but not very much. The portfolio still has a basic market value, and the discount might even serve as a cushion in a down market.

Look at the possibilities of investing in discount bonds for a good current return and capital gains. Also, income shares of the dual-purpose funds selling at discounts offer high return and capital-gains prospects. To get an idea of the earnings capability of a company, evaluate a stock on the basis of return over a period of time. In other words, what is the company capable of earning? Don't put too much emphasis on a steady growth pattern. If you do go into a growth stock with a high price/earnings multiple and a flat quarter comes up—panic, because everybody else will.

Don't rely too heavily on your broker. His job is to move stock, and he makes his living from commissions. Find a broker who will execute your orders and get your stock to you quickly and who will call back when you want him. When you make your own decisions, you can make mistakes, but at least you know your motives are to make money for you. Your broker wants to make money for himself and would like to make money for you. But even honest brokers cannot help having their judgment influenced, at least to some extent, by self-interest, and there are some who will churn you dizzy.

Be suspicious. If a broker calls you and suggests that you

buy a certain issue, chances are his firm is stuck with it and must unload it. You call him. Don't wait for him to call you.

I could bore you blind with historical studies and statistics that show that over the long run, stocks offer a better return on investment than bonds or money in the bank, but there have been more than enough figures in this volume. Let me just say that by its nature within the capitalistic system we have, equity (stock) must in the end pay more than debt (bonds) or the system breaks down. Businessmen who borrow and use the money in their business must earn a higher return on that money than they pay or else they go broke. If a retailer borrows money at 10 per cent to open a new store and that store returns only 9 per cent on the investment, it will have to close. There's no point in borrowing if you're going to lose money on the deal. More likely, if it's a viable operation he'll be earning 15 per cent or even 20 per cent. The stockholders will earn the difference between the cost of borrowed money and the return on it. In addition, stockholders will earn the full return on their equity money.

So in theory, stocks are better than bonds—the trick is to pick the right stocks at the right time.

After devoting an entire chapter to the invalidity of economic forecasts, it ill behooves me to make any predictions. However, barring too many exogenous developments, I predict that the American economy will survive, American business will grow (although perhaps not as rapidly as it did in the 1960's) and the stock market will remain an important investment vehicle. If I'm wrong, I'm prepared to submit to public ridicule and forfeit any right to time off for ill behoovior.

ACKNOWLEDGMENTS

Any book is the product of countless bits of information culled from who knows where, and it would be impossible to make proper acknowledgment to all who have contributed in some way. So I'll merely mention those who come to mind as having added so much that I could not in good conscience neglect a written word of thanks.

First to my wife, Adele, for her patience, criticism and occasional and necessary prodding. "Instead of watching another football game on TV, why not go upstairs and work?" still echoes in my ears. Next, my son, Allen, whose diligent research was responsible for the touch of class added by the references to the monetary affairs of classical civilizations.

Many thanks are due Peter Schwed and Sam Meyerson at Simon and Schuster, both of whom contributed conceptually to this project (that's authorese from "they gave me the idea for the book"), and my agent, Arthur Pine, for his unflagging enthusiasm—long may it wave.

Also to Len Lapidus and Art Samansky of the Federal Reserve Bank of New York, who did their best to unravel the mystery of central banking and fractional reserves for me. If they were unsuccessful, the blame rests here. To Pierre Rinfret I hereby submit thanks for the time he allotted me, accompanied by an apology for reviving that recession chestnut. Resisting temptation is not one of my strengths.

My secretary, Cynthia Nelson, must also be commended for helping when help was needed most.

Among the publications contributing mightily to my text were *The New York Times, The Wall Street Journal* and *Barron's*. There was also a host of brochures, speeches and monographs of frightening erudition that were digested and translated. To list them would be an exercise in the transfer of tedium.

Finally, I should make it clear that in acknowledging assistance, there is no attempt to shift responsibility. That belongs to me.